The Faint Ringing of a Caravan Bell

Fulton Books
Meadville, PA

Published by Fulton Books 2022

ISBN 979-8-88505-260-3 (paperback)
ISBN 979-8-88505-261-0 (digital)

Printed in the United States of America

The Faint Ringing of a Caravan Bell

AN AFGHAN DAUGHTER'S ODYSSEY

Trina Kayeum Shahbaz

Fluent in English, Farsi, and French and knowledgeable in Pashto and Arabic, Trina Kayeum Shahbaz has always had a fascination with words and a passion for poetry. After completing her graduate studies at Columbia University, she pursued her desire for learning by teaching English, French, and Farsi at several universities in the United States and abroad. Her cross-cultural experiences were enriched by traveling in Europe, Africa, Central Asia, the Middle East, Latin America, and Southeast Asia. This is her Afghan American, bicultural, and one-of-a-kind story as she adjusts while traveling from East to West.

Thank you, Daddy Jaan,
for gifting me with unshakeable pride in my heritage
and for lifting and sustaining me through life
with beautiful poetry.

Contents

Acknowledgments

With much love and respect for my mother whose exemplary passion for learning has been an inspiration for my personal and professional growth;

A huge debt of gratitude to Thor for his unwavering brotherly love, time, and help in editing this memoir, spurring me on to share my odyssey;

With much love to my husband, Ahad, for his devotion, patient editing, and support throughout my journey of balancing complex roles of mother, wife, and writer;

With many thanks to my friend Professor Robert Webber for encouraging me to write my story and introducing me to the complicated world of publishing;

With much appreciation to Professor Hamid Naweed for his artistic design contribution; and

Last but not least, much heartfelt gratitude to my teachers at Emma Willard School for their monumental contribution to my education, empowering me to share this important part of my cross-cultural journey and cherished poetry, gifted to me by my father.

Preface

My relationship with my father was beyond special. Although our bond was profound, it was essentially rooted in the simple observation of my son, Kamran, who at the age of six remarked, "Grandpa listens, and he respects everyone."

The youngest of the Kayeum clan and in a role of having lesser clout, Kamran could probably easily identify with the popular Afghan saying,

سگ قافله باشی ، خورد قافله نه

Sagay qaafila baashee khurday qaafila nay

May you be the dog of the caravan but not the caravan's youngest

Listening sincerely to people of all ages, regardless of their gender, background, nationality, religious orientation, range of intellect or other differences, was an ingrained and effortless gift of my father. One always came away from him with a keen sense of dignity even if this came just from having been heard.

He always boosted my confidence by acknowledging my accomplishments to me and others. Sometimes he'd nudge my mother and make comments like, "Did you hear that?" or "What a question!" or "I detect something unique in this child!" It was his focused attention and abundant generosity that made him so approachable. He was ever-welcoming of my overtures to speak with him and always exuded genuine caring that permeated his very being and counsel.

I was born into a large family, and was quite shy; others always seemed to command the lead in discussion. My father recognized my reticence, and because of his insight into human dynamics, he managed to ingeniously draw me out. Early on, he detected my aptitude for languages, and because he chose me specifically to engage with him in this area, I felt honored and naturally gravitated toward him. What ensued over a lifetime, far from the usual din of family interference, were very special one-on-one interludes that forged a life-long relationship full of laughter, creativity, and love.

My discussions with my father were interspersed with pertinent poetry, popular proverbs, and widely prevalent sayings or expressions in Farsi, Pashto, Arabic, English, and even French. These conversations provided added meaning, solace, and perspective as I encountered the day-to-day gyrations of adolescence. The humorous and witty multilingual play on words across five languages enhanced our time together immensely. As we would break out into fits of laughter, I could tell that he was enjoying himself as much as I.

We never deliberately set out to discuss the cultural elements of language. Sometimes they never came up. Typically, they sprang naturally from the organic ebb and flow of conversations pertaining to concerns, interests, or a recounting of the day's ordinary routines. A simple question on either of our parts would trigger and unleash a conversation rich with cross-cultural analysis and the ardor of poetry.

Whenever I heard my father recite a line that particularly moved me, I would jot it down on a piece of paper and store it in a box for later perusal. Typically, writing the poem just once was all I needed to commit it to memory forever. To this day, they are seared in my mind, and I can summon and recite the lines *par coeur* wherever and whenever needed.

As a child, I relished the time spent with my father, and today, the child in me still misses his larger-than-life presence. I am bound forever to acknowledge, honor, and convey my appreciation and high regard for him because of his huge influence on me as reflected in this memoir. My only wish is that Dad were still with us to have seen this book come to fruition, since he was really the compelling force behind it. Much of my life has been defined by him, and I will always be grateful and forever indebted for the special attention lavished on me in our unique relationship of enduring impact and love supreme.

Author's Notes

This story is about my cross-cultural journey across eleven time zones and three continents, which has lasted a lifetime. In it are interspersed favorite poems recited to me at pertinent times by my father. These add dimension and meaning to my experience. My journey starts in Afghanistan, where I was born and grew up, and brings me, years later, to my final destination in America. This odyssey is replete with cross-cultural observations, adjustments, personal challenges, and growth.

Although poetry and translation are an important part of this work, they serve as a vehicle to enhance the larger story and main focus on my years in a US boarding school. Some background on the important topic and role of poetry in my life is worthy of note.

Many have analyzed the vast oceans of Farsi poetry. Whereas I am not a poet myself, I grew up bilingual in Afghanistan with Farsi as my native language and Farsi poetry as a pervasive cultural element. Indeed, much of the poetry was in the form of couplets, quatrains, or excerpts of much longer works, truncated and inserted appropriately into the daily conversations of ordinary citizens.

As is customary in Afghan culture, I very much enjoy quoting poetry in discussions with Afghan friends and always share this enthusiasm with my English-speaking friends as well. Poetry is a mighty and intrinsic element of daily discussions among Afghans, whose ability to invoke the rhythmical compositions of great litterateurs never ceases to amaze me. Listening to people recite lines ranging from idiomatic expressions and colloquialisms to quoting the more elaborate poetry of the greats was part of my everyday life. It provided me with a special lens through which to view, make sense of, cope with trials and tribulations, or to appreciate the wondrous matters of this life and the world. This perspective and joy afforded through poetry is what I hope to impart in this book.

The beauty of Farsi poetry is its laconic quality. For anyone seeking profound, distilled meaning through brevity, Farsi poetry is appealing. Never verbose, the crisp, compact lines, often studded with rich imagery and always packed with deep philosophical meaning and universal appeal, resonate with me. In the East, the value of brevity is expressed very succinctly in the following:

قليل لفضى كثير معنى

Qaleelo lafzi, katheero mana

Few words, great meaning

Through deliberate economy of words and with adherence to very strict rules of form, the poets somehow manage to impart complexity and sophistication in matters of content, dispensed through profound pearls of wisdom without ever sounding either opaque or overly simplistic. Like great music, the lines are timelessly relevant. They heal or uplift, no matter what the experience of *la condition humaine* that I first came to learn about and analyze in my high-school French literature classes at Emma Willard.

The process of translating poetry has been paradoxically both onerous and enjoyable. Invariably, something gets lost in translation. The result is never perfect and the original is always incomparably finer. However, if one can accept this truth, translation is still meaningful, worthwhile, and even gratifying. It is a unifying force and the only hope for sharing this aspect of the world's wealth with one another.

Unlike other philosophies of translation, interpretation to me can often be a false representation and is, therefore, a transgression I consciously, diligently avoid. My intent is not to interpret but rather to translate the poet's words, leaving interpretation to the reader. Perhaps the biggest challenge for me has been to remain true to the original while capturing a measure of the melodic beauty of rhythm and rhyme wherever possible. Because I have kept the integrity of the verses intact, my conscience is clear, and the moral imperative to honor and respect the words of each great poet is upheld. Throughout this work, every effort has been made to give credit to the poets, although the names of some were irretrievable. No name below a couplet or a phrase means I was unable to identify the author. Further, proverbs and sayings are often passed on from generation to generation as valuable sayings or words of wisdom without being recorded in annals or books. With the exception of a few Pashto ballads, all the poems are in Farsi. There are a few Arabic sayings and phrases as well. Quranic quotes are notated as Scripture.

This book is not merely a story of cultural adjustment but a window into Afghan culture and language. My hope is that the centricity and significance of poetry in addition to my experiences in Afghanistan and the US will be of interest to both Afghans and Americans alike.

I. Farewell

1. Departure

When I was a child, people complimented me on my eyes. Like many Afghan girls, mine were brown and almond-shaped, but they were also very large. Always curious and interested in my surroundings, and not wanting to miss anything, I used to observe transpirings, wide-eyed and penetratingly, for long periods without blinking. This made my eyes glisten like the watchful ones of a cautious vigilant doe rather than of her playful, frisky little fawn. With all that I had witnessed and experienced in life up to this point, I was sedate and mature well beyond my years.

Departure day arrived in August of 1970 when I was just fifteen years old. My family bustled to Kabul airport where I was bound for the US to finish high school at Emma Willard School, an all-girls boarding school in Troy, New York. Feeling overwhelmed after many goodbye hugs and kisses, I boarded the plane. Although excitement about my future had been building up, I was unprepared to deal with the imminent severance from a life I had always known. The day of departure was more devastating than I could ever have imagined.

Some music I had recently heard streamed into my mind. It was my favorite of all of Rachmaninov's classical masterpieces. Now, the strains of his piano concerto no. 2, fresh in my memory, played dramatically in my mind as I stared out the window of the plane. My eyes welled up with tears that I had managed not to shed during the earlier farewells but now flowed down my cheeks like rivers. A Farsi poem, recited by my father, could approximate, although never fully express, the magnitude of my emotions on this day. It probably emanated from a place of pain for him as well, which he protectively shielded me from:

چشمی و خون در آستین، اشکی و طوفان در بغل   دارم دلی، اما چه دل، صد گونه حرمان در بغل

Daaram dilay amaa chi dil, sad goona harmaan dar baghal
Chashmay o khoon dar aasteen, ashkay o toofaan dar baghal

I have a heart but what a heart, a hundred sorrows in my chest
Blood-filled tears stream from my eyes, erupting like a typhoon in my breast

—Qudsay Mashhady

The exquisite Russian music, with its wide range of soft, lilting, deep, and rolling repetitive scales in true Volga style, played over and over in my head as the tears continued to stream uncontrollably down my face. I was flooded with a barrage of simultaneous mental images and bittersweet thoughts which animated the emotional intensity and sense of loss I was experiencing. I became a bit self-conscious of my tears lest anyone should take notice. However, supportive of my behavior, I thought:

خنده بر آن دیده که اینجا نشود گریان !   بردیده من خندی که اینجا ز چه میگرید

Bar deeday man khandee ki eenjaa zi chi maygiryad
Khanda bar aan deeda ki eenjaa nashawad giryaan

You laugh at my eyes, wondering why is she crying
Blast those eyes that would rebuke crying here!

—Khaqani

For the duration of my trip out of Afghanistan, to my final destination in New York, I was having myriad flashbacks of people and places throughout my childhood. These memories darted in my mind in no particular order as I became increasingly overcome by emotions. While waiting for take-off, my thoughts drifted to unforgettable experiences that at the time I did not know would never be encountered again.

No more visits with my cousins; no more Friday picnics to resorts like Paghmaan, Istaalif, Kaarayzay Meer, or the Qargha lake; no more eating meals in my favorite, most picturesque spot in all of Kabul, Baaghay Baalaa (Garden-Up-High), whose castle seems out of some fairytale or dream, perched like a jewel on a mount and nestled in Kartay Parwaan, surrounded by gardens of natural beauty; no more donkey rides or rides in horse-driven carriages or *gaadees*; no more idyllic trips to the provinces; no more drives to Day Baghalak, my father's birthplace and village, and his adobe childhood home or *qalaa*, a fort similar to the medieval castles; no more on the way to the great gorge would we be gazing in awe at the nomadic (Koochee) caravans in the distance, with their babies securely tied and bound, bobbing up and down atop huge, lumbering camels, making their long, slow journey in the wide-open desert to warmer southern spaces.

One of many picnics with family and friends.

The steep, sinuous road of the Tangay Ghaaroo gorge near Kabul.

Dad in his early forties in front of his family's *qalaa* in Laghman.

I would wonder and marvel at what it was that propelled these nomads to continually move forward with such strength, discipline, and determination despite the rugged terrain and harsh life.

On the way eastward to Laghman, my father's birthplace, we would travel through the beautiful sinuous Tangay Ghaaroo gorge with its sky-high, jagged mountains on all sides. Occasionally, we would stop and stretch while some of us would climb up and perch ourselves atop huge boulders by the roaring, twisting river paralleling the road.

No more, I reminisced, would we gobble down the scrumptious cold lunch of delicious lightly salted boiled eggs, potatoes, and savory seasoned chicken by the roadside as we dipped our toes in the refreshing water of the rushing river.

And finally, forlornly, no more would I be able to travel through a time tunnel into the past and excitedly experience the Laghmani way of my family's rich, rural history and culture. Everybody there lived in the same way as they had for generations before. Anytime we visited, it was as if time had stood still, and nothing had changed. How fun it always was for us children to experience life in this province that was so different from ours in Kabul.

The plane for some reason was delayed. My mind wandered from fragmented recollections to capturing memories of basic senses of my days in Kabul and its environs. There was the heavenly aroma of daily freshly baked naan, rising from naan baa-ees or bread bakeries, which appetizingly permeated the air each morning, noon, and evening. The process of making naan is quite involved. First, the dough is developed overnight. The following day, it is thinly stretched and spread over special firm pillows which are covered with nonflammable material, and the dough is sprinkled with either sesame or black seeds. The pillows are then lowered into a hot, deep underground tandor (oven) using long metal rods with forked ends, and they are slapped onto the scorching sides of the tandor where the dough is released and begins to bake, emitting an appetizing aroma of toasted seeds. When it is fully baked, just seeing and smelling the crispy thin slabs of naan, all neatly piled into warm stacks and ready for sale, arouses eager anticipation for dinner in all who pass by.

My sense of smell in Kabul was also frequently piqued by the sweet, powerfully intoxicating scent of roses, narcissi, orange blossoms, and cascading blooms in public and private gardens. Within most of these Shangri-las, gurgling streams flowed generously, and I wondered if they would ever trickle as lightly and playfully again around little stones, or if birds would chirp as sweetly around them in the morning or evening chorus.

"Alas," I mourned internally, "foregone pleasures galore about my homeland could go on forever!"

2. Remembrances of Laghman

Of all the places in Afghanistan, some of my fondest memories were of my ancestral home, Laghman. Scenes of this rural paradise flashed through my mind as my thoughts continued. Laghman was a magical place where life continued to play out as it had for centuries. It was a spot rich with a long family history and

اساطير الاولين

asateer al awaleen

long-ago ancient tales

Upon arriving at my father's *qalaa* fortress, we were always welcomed with unconditional love by Bobo Jaan, my ninety-year-old grandmother, who would hobble laboriously, approaching us with outstretched open arms from across a big reception room. She was always visibly and genuinely overjoyed to see us, and when she grew nearer, she would gently cup each of our faces between both hands and kiss our foreheads, saying repeatedly, *Bala dee wakhlam!* (Let me assume all ills and dangers that could possibly befall you.)

In her earlier days, Bobo Jaan was a great source of joy and entertainment for her children since there was no media of any kind in Laghman—no electricity, so no radio, movies, or television. At bedtime, her captivating storytelling, for which she had a high-standing reputation in the village, surpassed any diversion or fun that media could offer. By interspersing animating onomatopoeias for special effects throughout her storytelling, she would transcend all obstacles of communication, overcoming any deficiencies by creatively managing to generate her very own renditions for her children's amusement.

She was particularly gifted. One of my father's favorite stories was her dramatization of the night that a mighty dragon struck Day Baghalak, the very village where my grandfather's *qalaa* was located. My father recounted that since he and his siblings would soon be going to sleep there, the suspense was all the greater and almost more than the children could bear. As she spun the story full of intrigue, he and his siblings huddled and shuddered with utter fear and absolute delight at the scenes she created through sheer sound. The kids would cry out in terror as she waved her arms threateningly about and her heavy Pashto voice hit this crescendo:

پوښنهاری د ښنامار!

غورهاری د اسمان!

شرهاری د باران!

Pukh kha harrrray!" di khamar
(roared the fire-spewing dragon)

"Ghor rra harrrray!" di asman!
(rumbled the tumultuous falling sky!)

"Shar rra harrrray!" di baran!
(down poured the torrential deluge of rain)

Our Bobo Jaan in Laghman wished for the utmost safety and happiness for all of her more than twenty-five grandchildren. By the standards of many Afghans—and by hers, too—this entailed a long-standing tradition of cousins marrying cousins, a practice tested over and over through many generations. For most people, it was concluded to be the best plan for the well-being of all in the families concerned. My parents, who were more influenced by Western notions of love, marriage, and the need for gene pool diversity, raised their children on the premise that cousins were like brothers and sisters.

These novel ideas, however, were alien to Bobo Jaan who, at the age of ninety, was set in her ways and wasn't about to change her mind. Since she did not speak much Farsi, she did not say much to us on the subject, but she had mastered one line through which she tried to plant her thoughts in our young minds. It was personally relevant to her perspective and supported her point of view on the subject of finding a mate and marriage. She recited it during a reunion in Laghman when she had the forum and our full attention. With a mischievous twinkle in her eye, she mockingly denounced her children's and grandchildren's culturally divergent penchant for what she construed to be the pursuit of a more dubious "modern" perspective. She dramatized her point by stepping into our "misguided" lives, and with the familiar sarcastic little sparkle and thick Pashto accent, she would claim,

آب در کوزه و من تشنه لبان میگردم   یار در خانه و من گرد جهان میگردم

Aab dar koza o man tushna labaan maygardam
Yaar dar khaana o man girday jahaan maygardam

Water is in the jug and with thirsting lips I am roaming,
Love is here at home and I am round the world a-wandering

*****

Inspired by what we observed in Laghman and throughout early childhood, my younger sister Nina, my brother Thor, and I invented games in an effort to role-play and identify with the poor in the provinces. Sitting cross-legged on the floor, we would put aside forks and knives, which we used in Kabul, and instead, more authentically, use our hands to eat as we pressed our thumbs and forefingers together and pinched up the food, being ever so careful, as was the custom, not to spill or waste any or make a mess. The more we practiced, the better equipped we'd be for our next rendezvous with the reality in Laghman. We conducted conversations comprised of nonsensical made-up words like *makala...makala*, trying to replicate the Pashto language and provincial setting. As we conversed with one another in our imaginary tongue, we would eat gratefully and with gusto, just like the simple peasants we had observed.

It was so much fun to experience this simple life without all the utensils and modern amenities of electricity and plumbing in the more elaborate kitchens and bathrooms of Kabul. Marya once countered her American friend who bragged about her fancy bathroom in the US, complete with its ornate sink basin, pretty tiled shower walls, and three-way mirrors. In an effort to top her friend's boasting and win the one-upmanship competition, my sister retorted, "Oh, yeah? Well, you know in Laghman, the whole garden is my bathroom!"

How I loved it when my siblings and I would sleep peacefully at night with relatives, side by side, on the many *toshaks* or thin mattresses that were spread out, stretching across the entire floor of the very spacious dining room, now turned into a bedroom. It had a very high ceiling supported by large wooden beams, giving it grandeur, and to us, a peaceful sense of security.

By day, we were full of mischief, disrupting the work of the local farmers by climbing up and then sliding down huge, neatly piled haystacks without a worry in the world. Or we would balance ourselves on single logs as we traversed the large stream that flowed across the entire family's property.

We loved hacking the fresh sugarcane that grew everywhere in the lowlands, sucking out the sweet, satisfying nectar. After playing and running all day long around the land surrounding the *qalaa*, we would return to its center to drink the popular refreshing plain yogurt, cucumber, and mint drink known in the provinces as *shlombay*, packed with vitamins and known to have natural sedative qualities. Exhausted, we would then collapse on the open, raised dry mud terrace, which was lined with *toshaks* and soft big pillows. There, under the shade and dense canopy of fresh grapevines, to the mesmerizingly repetitive, soft chopping sound of the *paiko* or water-run nearby mill, we would drift off to sleep for a much-needed afternoon nap.

Everything seemed better in Laghman than in Kabul. Even *shlombay*, or *dogh* as it was known in Kabul, tasted more delicious in Laghman and quenched our thirst in this much hotter, dryer climate. We spent most of our time outdoors, running around the *qalaa* and grounds freely, unencumbered by any safety worries that usually concerned us in the big metropolis of Kabul. Whenever on the way to our provincial refuge, or whenever my father saw the new moon, no matter where he would be, he would often recite a couplet that described the peaceful bucolic scene in Laghman and the serenity of his childhood:

مزرعهٔ سبز فلک دیدم و داس مهٔ نو   یادم از کشتهٔ خویش آمد و هنگام درو

Mazray sabzay falak deedam o daasay mahay now
Yaadam az kishtay khaysh aamad o hangaamay darow

A green field of the Heavens I saw and a sickle-shaped new moon
Was reminded of the field I had sown and the time to harvest soon

—Haafiz

Grandmother Bobo Jaan with Dad, Thor, and cousin Bilqees

Sliding down a haystack in Laghman with Marya, Nina, and Homaira.

Crossing over a stream on our property:
Marya, cousin Baba, Homaira, Thor, I, and a turbaned villager.

Nina and I watching with fascination as *qalaa* women cook dinner.

Rest area under a cool fresh canopy of grapevines in the *qalaa* garden where children and adults relaxed, ate, drank *dogh* and tea and napped.

Dad forever connecting with fellow Afghans in the provinces.

A mother, likely in her teens, in one of the provinces.

3. Lingering Memories

My thoughts shifted from the lovely bucolic scenes in Laghman to sweet memories of childhood in Kabul.

No more would I frequent a movie theater with my sisters and younger brother for our one and only weekly dose of Western entertainment in the big city. Growing up, we had no television, so going to the movies was a cherished occasion. In the theater, to be shielded from potential unsavory characters, we would be flanked by two strong older cousins turned bodyguards. They created an impenetrable, protective barrier, and we felt completely confident that no harm could possibly befall us while enjoying the slice of Western life unfolding before us.

Every day, I enjoyed tuning into Kabul radio to listen to programs with renditions of sitar music which were interspersed with beautiful recitations of Farsi poetry, usually delivered by women with lilting, provocative voices. I also listened to my favorite nightly program, *Moozeek, Moozeek, Moozeek*, which featured Western pop and jazz artists like Duke Ellington, Ella Fitzgerald, Nat King Cole, Elvis Presley, and the Beatles. In hit songs, universal themes such as urgency ("It's Now or Never"), betrayal ("A Blossom Fell"), rapture ("Fascination"), nostalgia ("Yesterday"), helplessness ("Help!"), and peace ("Let It Be"), appealed to me greatly. I listened to this program religiously each night as I drifted off to sleep because it connected me to others in the far and wide world.

After the rare movie, during the balance of the week we enjoyed varied activities to amuse ourselves and pass the time. There were always adorable babies around that Nina and I cuddled and smothered with kisses. They eliminated any need for plastic dolls. We would march around the neighbors' yards, coddling the babies in our arms as if they were our own, talking to them and pretending to be their mommies. Their mothers had many tiring daily chores such as laborious hours of handwashing clothes in large earthenware (*taghaaras*) while sitting on their haunches in the courtyards. Or they would tediously comb or sieve—with their fingers—the daily family portion of dry rice, thinly spread out on platters, to remove possible impurities. After sorting and ridding the rice, grain by grain, of all unwanted particles, such as tiny stones and clumps of dirt, they would rinse it. Then they would soak it in cold water for several hours, allowing each grain to expand to its maximum size. An hour or so before dinner, they would boil the rice to prepare it for cooking. After oil and spices were added, it was finally ready for baking. *Et voilà!* By the time it was ready to eat, each grain was plumped up to the perfect desired size of half an inch or so in length.

In Afghan cuisine, there are many types of rice dishes, all requiring different spices, ingredients, and boiling and baking times. The variety and quality are on par with the best outputs of a Cordon-bleu chef. I always wondered how on earth these women could yield such a perfect platter every time without ever using any measuring or timing devices. It was taken for granted that with all their practice most women could put out a flawless spread practically with their eyes closed. This capability is tied up with their identity as proud cooks. They are always mindful to avoid potential blows to their ego by producing embarrassing outputs of bad food. It would not be possible (as they exclaim of themselves and their spread) that

نان بشرمد و ما نشر میم!

Naan bisharmad o maa nasharmaym!

the food be shameful and we not be shamed!

22

Women worked hard and steadily but competently and calmly. At times, they would use shortcuts such as pinching up items that were strewn on the floor with their toes rather than wasting energy by constantly bending down to reach them. But they always made time for tea breaks and socializing. In fact, if they detected their children were overexerting themselves or working excessively, they might admonish them with this motto supporting the Aristotelian concept of "golden means," albeit stated more plainly:

کاری بکو به اندازه   که ترا از پا نه بندازه!

Kaaray biko ba andaaza
Ki tura az paa nabindaaza

Do your work to a calculated degree
So that knocked off your feet, you will not be!

In general, achieving balance in life is encouraged while excesses in behavior are considered character flaws. A loftier Arabic phraseology appeals to the more educated of the population:

خیر الامور اوسطها

khairol omoor owsatuha

Good lies in the middle

Mothers were always happy to let us look after their little ones so they could have a break to attend to all their other duties. However, this was neither irresponsibly nor begrudgingly done. They always had the presence of mind to keep track of their children without ever spoiling our fun. Later, unlike all the "helicopter hovering" of children in America, I wondered how Afghan mothers could be so relaxed and trusting of other children to look after theirs.

My siblings and I spent hours with cousins, playing sundry card games, long-lasting games of chess, and heart-pounding, even heart-throbbing games of hide-and-seek in all the nooks and crannies of my uncle's big home.

One simple competitive childhood game, called "I remember and you forget," required good memory skills. It entails cracking a chicken wishbone between two people. The game involves giving and receiving of an object. Each time the giver hands over something to the receiver, he or she has to say, "I remember," If the person does not say, "I remember," the giver says, "I remember and you forget," which ends the game. Sometimes, the game would go on back and forth in this manner for days until one of the players would finally accept something without remembering and lose the game. Then everyone would laugh jokingly at the loser's poor power of retention.

When we were a bit older, we enjoyed the more sophisticated, competitive memory game called "poetry warfare." No doubt, this game was born from the importance accorded to poetry by most Afghans. Poetry is quoted in everyday conversations to support, illustrate, underscore, or legitimize any point in an argument or discussion. Almost everyone recites a poetic line or makes reference to a popular proverb or saying. This linguistic enhancement is deployed by all seasoned conversationalists. It is part of a national identity, a kind of expression of solidarity among countrymen.

The game involves taking fast turns, recalling, and speedily reciting elaborate lines of the great Farsi poets. Each person's turn begins with rattling off a verse that begins with the last letter of the previous person's line of poetry. The person who can quote a line when others can no longer think of one is the winner.

Zamaray, a brilliant older cousin, was particularly talented at poetry warfare. When we all ran out of options, he would often compose and then recite his own creations, trying to pass them off as classic poetry. Zamaray had a great command of the Farsi language, and his creativity often fooled us. Sometimes, though, we would catch him on his chicanery and call him out, yelling that he had made this or that line up. Half the fun of playing the game with him was in challenging him. When he would finally accept our protests and acknowledge his transgression, the rest of us would boisterously burst out into whopping, rollicking fits of triumphant laughter. The center of any gathering, Zamaray was charismatic, always so much fun and entertaining to be around. We loved it when he would take the time to play with us even though we were considerably younger and less knowledgeable than he. We knew he was doing this bunch of pipsqueaks a big favor by taking time to engage with us even though we were not part of his inner circle of friends, and we always appreciated the "adult" attention he bestowed upon us.

4. Innocence Lost

Peering through the small plane window, I craned my neck as far as I could to get another glimpse of my beloved cousin Homaira who was standing on the airport tarmac, fervently waving her hand at the departing plane. In those days, special escorting parties were allowed to accompany passengers all the way to the stairs of the plane. I was stunned by the gravity of severance and the paralyzing enormity of an unknown future flooded my mind. I summoned some words of wisdom, which partially appeased me:

کس ندانست که سرمنزل مقصود کجاست   اینقدر است که بانگی جرسی می آید

Kas nadaanist ki sar manzilay maqsoud kujaast

Eenqadar ast ki baangay jarasay mayaayad

No one knoweth where destiny lies,
This much, one can tell: the faint ringing of an approaching caravan bell

—Haafiz

Finally, the plane began to crawl forward and slowly picked up speed. In a few moments, the inevitable departure was well underway. Soon, my thoughts were interrupted by anything *but* the hint, lilt, or encouraging faint ringing of a caravan bell. The wheels of the airliner eventually screeched jarringly and loudly slammed under the fuselage with finality as the plane jolted abruptly upwards. The image of Homaira standing on the pavement fast faded and in a few seconds, became a mere speck until soon she disappeared altogether. I turned around in my seat and faced forward toward the direction the plane was moving although my mind still lingered on Homaira's image. Unsuccessfully, I tried to fight back more tears. They flowed down my cheeks, forming damp spots in my lap, as the rivers of my mind continued to spew a panoramic picture almost too enormous to scale down.

Not wanting to focus any further on departure, my thoughts returned to life in Kabul. What a jolly person and bosom buddy Homaira had always been and how unconditionally inviting, loving, and always accommodating were her parents—my uncle and aunt. In their house, we could do no wrong. We would turn the rooms topsy-turvy with our games of hide-and-seek and never be met with a harsh word of reproach. If a mess was made, food spilled or a glass accidentally broken, my Auntie Nafas Gul would unconditionally let us off the hook as she would calmly and lovingly repeat the customary saying of elders: "*Khair ast* (never mind; it's okay; no worries). *Sadqayt shawam* (may I be sacrificed for you)*!*" as she cleaned up, benevolently giving us assurance and a guilt-free conscience that no harm was done.

Everyone knew the following truism in Afghanistan, but my aunt, usually with a house full of kids to deal with, lived it like no other:

از خوردها لخشیدن ، از کلانها بخشیدن

Az khurdhaa laqsheedan, az kalaanhaa bakhsheedan

The youngsters slip, the elders forgive

It was no wonder how very dear my aunt was, not only to us but also to my Uncle Aaghaay Gul, who could not bear to be away from her for long. Their relationship was one of devotion and their love, very deep and special. She was to my uncle, as he would call her, his *nafas*—his soul and his every breath. We would never

27

again experience quite such a magnanimous or selfless love as from our Auntie Nafas Gul. More than anyone I had ever known, she embodied:

آنچه خوبان همه دارند تو تنها داری   بی سبب نیست که در دلم جا داری

Aanchi khoobaan hama daarand too tanhaa daaree
Bay sabab nayst ki dar dilam jaa daaree

That which all good people have, you alone possess
It is not for no reason that a place in my heart, you possess

—Shahriyar

During sleepovers, Homaira and I would stay up late, talk, joke, giggle, and snuggle under the same large comforter, known as a *lee-aaf*. In winter, we pulled the billowing layers up to our chins to keep warm, and would tell each other jokes. Whether lying on the floor on a *toshak, mattress* or later, on a *chaar-paa-ee*, the four-legged version of a modern bed, we snuggled under the same *lee-aaf*, laughing at funny stories of people, events we had witnessed in school, and sharing secrets and dreams for a life of greater fulfillment in a more open, free, and modern society. In our connection and comradery, problems would vanish into the night air.

Like most Afghans, during the winter months, Homaira and I spent many long hours, keeping warm in the main family room of her home, under the voluminous blankets of a *sandalee*. The *sandalee* consisted of a small metal heater full of burning charcoal, placed carefully under a big square table over which several comforters were spread. These dangled on all four sides, covering and warming the legs and laps of all those sitting around the table. It was on soft *toshaks* backed with firm supporting pillows placed around the *sandalee* that we would spend many cozy hours chatting, laughing, shelling and consuming handful after handful of pine nuts and pistachios, drinking tea, and playing card games.

As bittersweet memories of childhood and my soulmate continued to pass through my head, feelings of uncertainty about the future increased. An ominous sense emerged that making such a close friend as Homaira would be extremely difficult, if not impossible, in America.

Homaira dressed up in national costume

Nina and I in uniform on the way to school.

The pilot interrupted my thoughts with an insignificant announcement. My memories were replaced by a need to contemplate my present predicament. Whether the daughters of ordinary citizens or diplomats, young girls never traveled anywhere alone at the age of fifteen, let alone all the way from Afghanistan to America. I can recall that in all of Afghanistan, there were only two other girls who alone, in their late teens, were sent to the US for academic studies. They were our friends, and like us, had American mothers.

Although girls in Kabul were allowed to freely attend all levels of education, the selection and quality of schools available in Afghanistan were quite limited, especially compared with those in the US. In addition to strong points in Afghan education and culture, our parents tried hard to expose us to a rich variety of elements such as western drama, classical music, and dance which were otherwise missing in a typical Afghan child's life. Homeschooling to fill in all the gaps was a difficult task for my mother and the other few American mothers married to Afghans.

With a mixture of apprehension and optimism, I finally derived pride, albeit perhaps falsely, in predicting victory in my departure. Soon, with the power of autosuggestion, I became determined to succeed in whatever destiny lay before me. Although traveling with three siblings was consolation, I knew it would be short-lived since upon arrival in New York, we all would go our separate ways to different schools. I enjoyed the last few days I had on this trip in their company. We talked about the imminent change to come in our lives, and I listened intently to the advice and reassurances given by Rona (20) and Marya (18) on adjusting to schools and life in the U.S. Rona was on her way to becoming a junior at Middlebury College in Vermont. Marya had just graduated high school from Dana Hall School in Massachusetts and was on her way to college in Rochester, New York. Thor, who was fourteen, was about to begin high school at Phillips Exeter academy in

New Hampshire. He did not appear to be phased at all by leaving Afghanistan and not looking back, he showed eager curiosity about all aspects of this new adventure. What we all shared was that we would resume our studies in the US although in different states. The thought of this separation was a bit unsettling, but I continued to use my best coping skills to leapfrog into a strong, "can-do" mentality as I girded myself for the upcoming reality of yet another separation. I tried not to dwell on this but instead imagined how nice my new life might turn out to be.

However, optimism and confidence were not outcomes that could be easily willed into existence, especially when there were so many vastly abstract unknowns. Some familiar paradoxically consoling and foreboding words of origin that my father sometimes recited, describing primordial insecurity, came to me. As I had just left my country of birth, numerous tensioned vacillations between my known past and an unknown future arose, but mentally I returned to the certain comforts of childhood and home, remembering:

طفلی و دامان مادر خوش بهشتی بوده است   تا به پای خود روان گشتیم سرگردان شدیم

Tiflee o daamaanay maadar khush biyhishtay booda asst
Taa ba paay khud rawan gashtaym sar gardaan shudaym

Infancy and Mother's bosom such heavenly bliss as one and the same
'Twas when we walked on our own, lost we became

—Baydil

*****

My thoughts returned to pleasant times of more peace and security. Other than going to my uncles' homes, or on a few outings, we led a protected and sheltered life in Kabul, spending virtually all of our time at school or at home within our yards and compounds.

Coming from a prominent, extended family of patriarchs, all of whom at one time or another held high political positions such as Minister of Health, Head of Parliament, Prime Minister, Advisor to the King, Commandant of Kabul Forces, Governor of Kapisa Province, Governor of the Helmand Province, Minister of Information and Culture, Minister of Interior, Minister of Education, and Deputy Prime Minister, we were not free to come and go as we pleased or visit friends' homes. Fraternizing outside the family was not considered safe, and without proper chaperoning, we did not leave the house.

The three prominent patriarchs: (left to right) Uncle Aaghaay Gul, Uncle Shahlaalaa, and Dad.

The lack of outside stimulation made us dig deep within for entertainment. With our real and invented games, we were never bored. It's telling that the word *boredom* does not exist in Farsi. Two words, *khasta* and *dil-tang,* come close but are not quite the same since the former has a more physical connotation of being tired and the latter, of being restless. In Emma Willard, I read one of Emerson's essays in which he expounds on the power of the imagination and one's ability of "taking a trip in the mind." In Afghanistan, this was a common practice.

Most of the time we were required to study so much that we had to find a way to make it palatable. Nina turned study time into a diversion, and with her rich imagination, she made up an elaborate game. On the family blackboard, she would scribble her lessons, learning them by imagining she was a teacher in front of a class of students. In this process, she would execute all of her well-designed, imagined classroom procedures in great detail. She would conduct complete role-plays, full of live conversations with her imaginary students, whom she called on by name. She even had a gradebook in which to record their performance and progress. In the course of these classes, she would sometimes take on the part of the teacher and sometimes that of a student. Often, she would throw into these imaginary classes that she conducted at home, her own real school experiences full of teacher comments and admonitions that she had heard in her actual class at school.

What was truly humorous about all of this was that she managed to fool our house help, Khairudeen, who thought that real school was in session. On one occasion, we all burst out laughing when my mother asked Khairudeen to fetch something from a room that required his passing by the blackboard.

"Oh, no!" he replied with awe and fearful respect. "Malim Saheb (Madam Teacher), Nina Jaan is conducting class there, and I've been commanded never ever to disrupt her lessons!"

The underlying beauty of simple folk in Afghanistan was incredibly charming and endearing. Often provincial lads had never been exposed to any aspect of modern life, and they came to Kabul to work in homes to complete a mandatory two-year draft in the army. They brought with them their charmingly innocent ignorance. My father often referred to the whole process as being akin to a transient "living museum." He had the wisdom and foresight to know how society was ever-changing and evolving, always encouraging us to observe, appreciate, absorb, and learn from these unique and fleeting experiences and moments in history. Once he described to us an occasion of total innocence when he was in a remote area in the provinces and parked his bicycle outside someone's *qalaa*. When he returned, he found a pile of hay and a bucket of water on the ground beside the front wheel of the bike. Assuming that the hay would nourish the bicycle, the villagers in this manner, demonstrated the ultimate expression of hospitality.

Another instance of charming innocence occurred when Khairudeen was asked to plug the iron into the socket to iron a shirt for my father. A look of terror came over him as he grew pale. He pleaded not to go near the outlet, claiming that the last time he did so, a scorpion was hiding there and had bitten him. Apparently, he attributed the electrical shock to a scorpion's sting.

Occasionally, for a taste of real life in Kabul, I would venture out with my aunt and her daughter, a married, much older cousin. Both experts at shopping and getting around the city, they were well familiar with the culture and how to handle themselves and others. I felt completely safe going out with them. They always knew exactly when and how to assert themselves so as to protect us from any mishaps. Sometimes, when unsavory males got too near, they would ward them off with preemptive retorts of disgust that other women used as well: "Hey, aren't you ashamed of yourself? Don't you have sisters or a mother of your own? Go away, go away, and give us space!"

Our little group would then confidently march into the crowded *saraays* or shopping alleys. They were full of little shops with all kinds of wares, from fresh and dried fruit to a vast array of seasonings neatly piled high in straw baskets to various items of clothing for sale, dangling in the front portion of shops. My aunt and cousin would begin the purchasing process with a masterful display of interaction between themselves and the shopkeepers. It was complicated, involving many steps of strategizing, bargaining, haggling, walking away, returning, walking away again, and always knowing precisely when to make the final return to ultimately buy the item at the lowest possible price. There was an art and science to this process, consisting of an astute psychological reading of people. A couple of times I tried to replicate their shopping strategy and became so confused that I wound up tongue-tied and embarrassed and inevitably failed, paying more than the item's original price.

A shocking outing just before I left Kabul for the States jolted me considerably. It happened under the safe wing of my aunt so the blow was not calamitous. The circumstance was during Aashura, a major day in Islam but particularly among Shia muslims. It is a time to observe probably the greatest of all Islamic tragedies, which occurred in Iraq after the death of the Prophet. The Prophet's grandchildren, Imam Hassan and Imam Hussein, whom Shias believe were the rightful heirs to the Islamic tradition, were murdered during the battle of Kabala. Their deaths are seen as the ultimate sacrifice, or martyrdom, for the sake of saving Islam from despotic oppression.

My aunt took me to a nearby religious center called a *takya khaana,* specifically designed for Ashura where in violent acts, shackled men walked about in circles, verbally lamenting and flagellating themselves with chains in remorse for the fate they wished they could have somehow averted. This continued until their backs and bodies were bloody from the self-inflicted flogging. Although quite disturbing to me, the experience was also strangely mesmerizing. I thought the bloody practice was unique only to Shias until years later in America when I witnessed similar behavior though for completely different reasons, portrayed by a medieval monk depicted in a Hollywood movie.

The small Ariana Airlines plane continued its ascent and then suddenly, more assuredly and definitively, jerked upward so as to clear the fast-approaching heights of the forever snow-clad mountain peaks of the Himalayan Hindu Kush. Soon, the ascent severed me completely from the view of Afghan terrain. The magnitude of my physical distance and separation seemed more like a disastrous defeat than an imagined achievement filled with pride. Foresight had not proven to be a forte of mine. My new reality brought to mind migration, signaling the point of no return. Often, my father, when gazing at a flock of birds fervently flapping their wings and flying in perfect formation in a single direction, would recite,

از گوشهٔ بامی که پریدیم ، پریدیم   دل نیست کبوتر که چو برخاست نشیند

Dil nayst kabootar ki choo barkhaast nisheenad
Az goshay baamay ki pareedaym, pareedaym

The heart is not some pigeon to take flight and then alight
From the corner of a rooftop we flew, forever out of sight

—Wahshy Baafiqy

This poem was later incorporated into a famous ballad by my cousin Ahmed Zahir, one of the greatest Afghan singers of all time. The lyrics became particularly relevant upon the mass displacement of Afghans during and after the Soviet invasion.

*****

37

When we reached the desired altitude, a flight attendant disrupted my thoughts by offering hard candy in a small straw basket. I couldn't pass up this opportunity. Despite my inner turmoil, I smiled thankfully, taking one while surreptitiously squirreling away a few more, as my smile probably transitioned from thankful to guilty. I remembered my mom who always tried to ensure the well-being of her children. To promote good dental and overall health, she rarely gave us sweets that I so often craved. I accepted this deprivation, rationalizing that, after all,

هر روز عید نیست که حلوا خورد کسی

Har roz Eid nayst ki halwaa khurad kasay

Not every day is Eid to be eating halva

Although the bazaars offered desserts such as sweet and salted cookies, sugary rosewater *firnees* (creamy purees topped with pistachios), rice puddings, fried crispy pastries sprinkled with powdered sugar as well as honey-drenched *jilabees*, we enjoyed all these only on special occasions when our family was invited out. Unfortunately, my favorite sweet, which was chocolate, was almost never available.

On very rare occasions, in an area called Day Mazang, when we passed by a specialty store that imported products from abroad, I would get a ration of one or two small squares of a Swiss chocolate bar that Mom would divide amongst herself and all of her kids. It always seemed that by the time my tongue touched it, it had already melted away and was gone. In a way, this was more torturous than if I had never been given any at all.

Once during Eid, my father gave my siblings and me each one entire chocolate bar. Savoring the entire bar all by myself felt like I had died and gone to heaven. Perhaps the next best thing to chocolate for me was *chukeeda*—a crushed mixture of the sweetest ground dried mulberries and walnuts, a particularly delicious combination yielding an incomparable gestalt of toasted flavor and sweet taste. Made without sugar, it was probably a lot healthier than chocolate bars, too. This treat was labor intensive and difficult to make, and therefore, not for daily consumption. Consequently, I always longed for more sweets. My father's love and craving of sugar closely aligned with mine. As I took a few more hard candies from the flight attendant's basket, forbidden desire and my father's boyhood mischievousness unfolded:

قند دزدی چقدر شیرین است

Qanday duzdee chiqadar shireen ast!

How much sweeter is the stolen sugar cube!

—Erij Mirza

From yearning for sweets during childhood, I wandered to the more severe scenes and examples of real deprivation in Afghanistan. Often, while driving with my father in the provinces on holidays, swarms of barefoot children, who had never seen a car, would run after ours, excitedly shouting greetings and salutations such as, "*Akhtar di mubaarak sha* (Happy Eid to you)!" I would crane my neck as far as I could after we passed them, trying to still see them through the car's trail of airborne dust, in an effort to somehow reconcile or atone for the financial disparity between us. I felt morally responsible to honor their meager existence and great effort, despite having nothing, in acknowledging us and being hospitable in their small corner of the world. The memory of these children lingered hauntingly in my mind long after their images faded. My father made us particularly aware of the poor, whose plight is sometimes glorified:

ما هیچ نداریم و غم هیچ نداریم

Maa haych nadaaraym o ghamay haych nadaaraym

We have nothing and have the worries of nothing

—Khwaaja Kermani

Empathizing with the poor as a young child, I would smuggle basic supplies of rice and flour, but mainly sugar, from our house to give to the needy. I took pleasure in knowing that I enhanced their plain dinner of bread and tea which was now spiked and sweetened with a generous serving of sugar as well. I enjoyed receiving verbal praise from the poor and always listened to their long eloquent religious blessings of thanks and appreciation. With all the have-nots in Afghan society, one could hardly escape the value of charity. The effects and awareness of hardship were deeply ingrained in the culture, religion, and the very ethos of the country. In his own gentle and subtle way, simply by spotting them, my father would often bring our attention to those less fortunate.

In school, subjects of theology, comportment, and Farsi literature all emphasized and reinforced consciousness of, and sensitivity to, the downtrodden:

تو نیکی میکن و در دجله انداز   که ایزد در بیابانت دهد باز

Too naykee maykun o dar dajla andaaz
Ki ayzid dar bee-aabaanat dihad baaz

Do good unconditionally, casting recognition by others into the river
So that whilst in the barrenness of your own desert, God might deliver

—Sa'adi

The flight attendant's candies helped to divert my serious thoughts. I uncovered one and quickly placed it in my mouth, chewing down hard on the crunchy outer portion all the way to the inner gummy, gooey center. Not having quite finished the first one, I quickly unwrapped another one and stuffed it in my mouth, too, for good measure. Chewing both over and over again, I tried not to swallow too quickly to fully savor the ephemeral burst of sweetness before its complete dissolution. It was as though by directing all my attention to the joyful experience of eating my candy and prolonging the sweetness, I found some psychological relief in the face of an uncertain future.

5. Fledgling Democracy

Juxtaposed with the intimidating predicament of traveling to the US were thoughts about the threatening political undercurrents of the past decade in Afghanistan. Although still a child, I was more than aware of the underlying and imminent dangers faced by the government and my father, who was Minister of Education at the time, as one of its cabinet ministers.

Afghanistan had always been a poor country but rich in national pride. Never being dominated by foreign intruders added to this sense of immense self-respect and identity. Mostly an agrarian culture, for centuries, it resembled Europe's feudal Middle Ages. Although not called serfs or slaves, many people served the *Khans,* the equivalent of medieval "lords," in exchange for financial support of room and board, but often with little or no extra compensation.

Over the years, like many other impoverished nations, Afghanistan became ripe for communist ideology with its focus on financial equity, land distribution, and promise of economic freedom. Communism never succeeded in taking hold at any point in Afghan history because Afghans are profoundly religious and are fiercely individualistic. Equating communism with Atheism, they could never accept its atheistic ideology. Although never technologically advanced, Afghans' unshakeable religious conviction always served as the greatest defense against any intruder.

Over time, communist influence with promises of justice and equality found its way to Kabul buttressed by Soviet era backing and meddling. Many of the dorms in high schools became fertile grounds to disperse communist ideology among the growing number of educated young people. Realizing this political threat to democracy and the financial drain of these schools on resources in Kabul, my father opted to persuade his colleagues to decentralize the high schools, sending boys back to their homes in the provinces. I remember him telling me about a proposal and solution to this problem he was to present in an upcoming cabinet meeting with the prime minister.

More prevalently than I was ever fully aware of as a young child, throughout my father's political career, there was the impending threat of communism and communist rule in Afghanistan. Even early on in his career, as governor of Helmand Province in the 1950s, he would listen through all the static of the radio to renditions of the news coming from Kabul for updates on Soviet activities. After Dad's ten-year service as governor, my family moved to Kabul in the early 1960s when he assumed the post of Minister of Information and Culture and then Minister of Interior. I became more aware of the growing political threat with the advent of the first demonstrations in the early 1960s.

Student demonstrators holding up pictures of communist party candidates in Kabul.

In the beginning, the demonstrations were peaceful, but once, without any explanation, we were held back at home from school for a whole week. One of the demonstrations had turned into a riot, and by the time the violence ended, a couple of students had been fatally shot. At the time, my father was the Minister of the Interior and would return home utterly exhausted after spending an entire day and night troubleshooting to keep the peace. At one point, as he and Prime Minister Yosuf, were going to the parliament, they were encircled by rioters. Dad began speaking to them in their primary language, Pashto, which impressed them favorably, and in doing so, he managed to dispel the mob and divert the threatened prime minister to safety.

The death of the two students was, unfortunately, pinned on my father, who was falsely accused of having given the order to shoot. The order, however, had been given by a high-ranking army officer and member of the royal family whose identity was intentionally never revealed. Since my father was in charge of the capital police department, he was scapegoated. Later, autopsies revealed that the bullets found in the slain student bodies were connected with ammunition belonging solely to the army, not the police force. The ordeal came to be known as the infamous "Say Aqrab" (the third day of the eighth lunar month). Shortly thereafter, the debacle resulted in a colossal government change, and in 1966 my family and I left for the United States for two years. This was perhaps the single most pivotal event in modern Afghan politics, which my father recognized as being the very beginning of the demise of his dream to establish democracy in the country under the shadow of the Communist threat.

We spent two brief years in the US before returning to Afghanistan in 1968. Those two years in the States were fraught with political unrest, culminating in the horrific assassinations of Martin Luther King and Robert Kennedy. Throughout this period, my siblings and I were obliged to adjust in different states to new schools and unfamiliar surroundings. Moving between continents and skipping grades to be current with our peers was disruptive and had ripple effects on our education. We seemed to always be scrambling to catch up academically both in the American and Afghan school systems.

During my last days in Afghanistan before I left for boarding school, my family was under fire in more ways than one. Student demonstrations were on the increase. The Communist Party and movement, led by Soviet-backed Babrak Karmal, was gaining momentum. In their efforts to spread communist ideology, they slyly twisted and manipulated Quranic language to appeal to the Afghan masses, who were Muslim. To make their dogma enticing, they coined Arabic slogans equivalent to catchy Marxist ones such as "Workers of the world unite. You have nothing to lose but your shackles." Their out-of-context Arabic phraseology would become,

الكاسب حبيب الله

Al kasib habib Allah

The worker is loved by God.

Once, the protesters and rebellious insurgents invaded the Parliament, disrupting routine official business. Again, the fledgling democratic government, of which my father was an integral member, was struggling to keep the situation peaceful. What started as a group of just a few communists began to grow, and students and the masses were increasingly being brainwashed. An Arabic quote that comes to mind about these people is this:

العوام كل انعام بل هم اضل

Al awam kal anam bal hum adal

The masses are like cattle but even worse.

46

The coerced "dumb-driven cattle" made matters worse with frequent uprisings that were turning violent. There were death threats directed at my family. My siblings and I were not told of these, but I knew something was radically wrong and strange. On one occasion, a dozen or so soldiers in full uniform marched into the front yard of our house with guns held rigidly at right angles to their sides, their flashing bayonets flung out, gleaming in the sun. The soldiers surrounded the house, aiming their guns at the yard's entrance.

On another occasion, my soft-spoken mother, who rarely raised her voice, after a call from my father, suddenly started giving my younger brother a tongue-lashing at high octaves that by now he ought to have known how to get his pants on, that he was no longer a baby, and that all of us were to be ready immediately to get into our Soviet-manufactured jeep, and duck our heads down until we got to my uncle's house for refuge. When we arrived at my uncle's house, my three older cousins were standing at open windows holding guns, all aimed at the yard entrance. They had been directed by my uncle to aim for the foot and shoot any and all intruders.

Later, during major rioting on another day, the boys from a nearby school stormed my high school to ridicule the principal and parade her around the courtyard, shouting insults. All order and classes were disrupted. They shattered the glass on the door to my classroom to get in. My French teacher tried to hold it shut. I shuddered for my fate if one of them should ask a classmate to identify the daughter of Dr. Kayeum. But in their impatient haste, by some miracle, they did not tarry long to struggle with the classroom door.

The entrance essay to Emma Willard, the boarding school I was currently bound for, was about this very riot and the storming of my high school. I was so happy and flattered that the admission personnel had liked it and had accepted me. It was confirmation that I had measured up to their high academic standards.

Increasing violence in Kabul posed a threat to the Afghan government, similar to that depicted in *Camelot*, a movie I had recently seen. King Arthur's round table being broken and violently smashed to pieces under the stomping hooves of horses and the dissidents who rode them flashed before my eyes. The hopes, dreams, and lifelong efforts of my father and his colleagues to develop and secure a liberal democracy in their beloved homeland was now subject to the same heart-wrenching imminent doom depicted in the tragic Camelot tale. Nevertheless, government officials worked patiently and tirelessly to avert total catastrophe. However, time was not on their side, as my father sardonically noted in the following analogy:

به این تمکین که ساقی باده در پیمانه می ریزد   رسد تا دور ما دیوار این میخانه میریزد

Ba een tamkeen ki saaqee baada dar paimaana mayrayzad
Rasad taa dowray maa, diwaaray een maikhaana mayrayzad

With such finesse and tedium this sommelier pours wine into the chalice
Til it is finally our turn, the very walls of this tavern will collapse

—Sufi Ghulaam Naby Ashqari

The end of a golden era in Afghanistan had been slowly approaching, and was now almost upon us.

In his last position as Minister of Education, my father often lamented that had the country not been so ravaged by misguided outside influences, he could have directed his attention more to its internal progress. Afghanistan could have benefited so much by building a better infrastructure and providing more and better educational opportunities for its citizens. Throughout his career, many positive changes in these areas had been made but of course there was still much to be desired. My father often referred to achieving his ultimate dream of transforming Afghanistan into an enviable "Switzerland of Asia," both in the aesthetic but also political sense of neutrality.

Without being afforded the opportunity to realize the full potential of democracy in the form of a constitutional monarchy, successive cabinets fell, leaders were forced to resign prematurely, and democratic governance in Afghanistan was impeded. The astute and brutal brevity of a Sufi saying connotes all things passing:

و آن ساقی نماند   آن قدح بشکست

Aan qadah bishkist
Wa aan saaqi namaand

The goblet shattered
And, that sommelier vanished

—Attar

All his fervent attempts to advise United States officials regarding matters they knew little about were summarily dismissed as mere Quixotic dreams by the US State Department "Afghanologists".

How ironic was it that, in 1968, as a family, we should see the magnificent musical, *Man of La Mancha,* our first-ever live stage production in Chicago just before we returned to Afghanistan. As I listened to the very moving songs, "To Dream the Impossible Dream," "Dulcinea," and "To Each His Dulcinea," whose lyrics I knew by heart, tears of empathy for worthy people who were not being taken seriously streamed down my face.

Shortly after this performance, we began the long journey home, making the most of limited family funds by sailing from New York to Dover, England, and then camping throughout Europe, all the way through Turkey and Iran, finally reaching Afghanistan. There, once again and for the last time, in his final official position, my father, with every fiber in his being, launched a fervent attempt to save his beloved country from disintegration. With all the destructive and divisive meddling of foreign forces still at play, he resumed once again, the Herculean task of (as he once put it), "putting Humpty Dumpty together again."

The inevitable failure, despite all efforts to thwart a catastrophic destiny for Afghanistan, brings to mind the long-ago repartee of two renowned poets on the subject of futility and despondency in life:

سحرگه وه د نرګس لیمه لانده ٮ۬ٛاسکی ٮ۬ٛاسکی یی د سترګو ٮ۬ٛتۧید ه

ما وي شکلی ګله ولی ژاړی ده وي دا ژوند دی یوه خوله خندیده

Saharga wa di nargis laymu laandu

Tsaaskay tsaaskee yay du sturgo tsutsaydu

Maa way shkulay gula walay zhaaray

Du way daa zhwand duy yowa khlu khandaydu

It was dawn when from the moist eyelids of a narcissus
One by one, teardrops trickled down from her eyes
I asked, "Lovely flower, why do you cry?"
She replied, "Such is life…one fleeting, momentary smile."

—Pashto Poetess Nazo Ana

Responding some 100 years later, the Farsi poet Iqbaal more boldly replied:

درخشید برق سبکسیر و گفت   شبی زار نالید ابر بهار

این دنیا گریهٔ پیهم است   نه خیر خطا کرده ای

Shabay zaar naaleed abray bahaar
Durukhsheed barqay subuksair o goft
Nakhair khataa karda-ee
Zindagee giryay paiham ast

The clouds of spring wailed misery in the night
A free-spirited lightning bolt flashed, declaring,
Nay, you are mistaken
Life is naught but weeping in perpetuity

—Iqbaal

After the disintegration of the Soviet Union in 1991, Afghanistan was reduced to tatters by civil war. Reflecting wistfully on his political career, my father would often agonize over how things could have been done differently to yield a more positive and sustainable outcome. A much-practiced but totally unacceptable alternative would have been to squelch the opposition dead in its tracks. The following adage is more akin to that way of thinking:

اقتل الموضی قبلا ایضا

Uqtul ul moozee qablan eeza
Kill the danger before it endangers you

However, this was an abhorrent concept to my father. Agonizingly, he once gave me his analysis of the complex nature of his predicament:

> *Could, somehow, some kind of better, benign strategy to pacify opposition have been implemented much earlier on to thwart the destructive efforts and effects of the initial very small number of communist insurgents or dissidents? And even if so, how could this catch-22 situation have been achieved without destroying the very tolerance any true democratic system must exhibit? But even more challenging and dangerous, how could an effective strategy have been put into play without any deadly violence ensuing?*

Resigned, he invariably came to the same fatalistic conclusion, reciting a simple verse connoting the ephemeral nature of all things temporal in politics, government, and beyond:

هر کسی پنج روز نوبت اوست

Har kasay panj roz nobatay ost

For each 'tis but a five-day chance

—Haafiz

During my last year in Kabul, as I dealt with my academic challenges and witnessed the Afghan political scene unravel, life sometimes seemed unrewarding. Although only fifteen and unaware of the full gravity and extent of the country's impending demise, the bits of information I managed to piece together often left me feeling overwhelmed by my father's difficult predicament.

The situation appeared more and more thankless, like the woman who diligently tends to the stewing pot, churning and churning it, all the while enduring the fumes from the burning embers below it:

نخوردیم از آشش ، کور شدیم از دودش

Nakhordaym az aashash kor shodaym az doodash

Ne'er did we consume the soup, but blinded were we by its smoke

*****

Finally, our plane landed in Tashkent, Uzbekistan. I was mentally exhausted as this part of my journey finally came to a close. The new surroundings in the Soviet Union caused my old memories to recede. When we disembarked, my siblings and I almost immediately felt the vibes of a threatening world. We underwent heavy scrutiny of our luggage at various checkpoints because of increased suspicion of drug trafficking. The border officials were officious and unpleasant, dumping out the contents of our bags and then stuffing them back in. We found this quite offensive since we were just a bunch of clean-cut kids who were passing through. Another jarring experience during this first stop was drinking carbonated water for the first time and hating the taste of it. However, in earlier childhood, I had been told never to take for granted the precious commodity of water as noted in Scripture:

وَجَعَلْنَا مِنَ الْمَاءِ كُلَّ شَيْءٍ حَيَّ

Wa ja-alna min alma-i kulu shai-in hai

We made from water every living thing

53

We then proceeded to our Moscow connection, where my siblings and I were met by Afghan government officials. They were very hospitable, offering us good Afghan food in their modest home and the refreshing, lightly salted *dogh* drink, with a more than generous amount of chopped cucumber in each glass. They took us to our first-ever ballet performance, at the prestigious Bolshoi Ballet Theater, which was unlike anything I had experienced in Kabul. I enjoyed the great Russian dancers who resembled the prima ballerina Plisetskaya whom I had seen on screen in Afghanistan. These dancers did not quite match up to her virtuosity or fantastical wave-like, double-jointed arm movements. Nonetheless, enjoying my first live performance in that very elegant setting was a very memorable experience. We sat in soft red velvet seats and watched as the elaborate shiny chandeliers dangling from the ceiling slowly dimmed and the performance began. The scene was reminiscent of Russia's historic royal opulence and of the movie *Dr. Zhivago* that I had recently seen. The Bolshoi experience was drastically different from the actual grim setting of the Communist regime outside.

A relief from Moscow's general austerity was walking on the very wide boulevards, purchasing and eating cookies and ice cream sold in little stands. This was very different from Kabul where we were not allowed to eat food sold on the street for fear of contracting dysentery. We walked around the Ukraina Hotel, where we were staying, ordering *chiteery* (four) of everything as we pointed to items we wanted to buy—one extra, in case any of us wanted to eat more but also because we didn't know how to say any other number in Russian.

We didn't understand why the Soviets didn't smile or look very happy, and being among them became increasingly unpleasant. After a few days in Moscow, we were relieved to finally get on the long flight to New York.

While we were in Afghanistan, through diplomatic channels, high-ranking Soviet officials had offered us full scholarships for undergraduate and graduate studies in Moscow. However, my father knew better and declined. At this point, I was so grateful that Moscow was not our final destination but that we were on our way to America instead to continue and consummate our academic studies.

6. The Malalai Malaise

After some sightseeing and walking up and down the boulevards, the remaining time in Moscow, I began to reflect with relief upon the challenges of my life in Afghanistan that I was humbled by and would be happy to leave behind. Circumstances had not been rosy the last few years either socially or academically, particularly at my high school, Malalai. Having spent a couple of years in the US due to the regime change in Afghanistan, which had made my father unable to work there, I returned to Kabul with my family and was lagging behind in school. I was focused primarily on my studies, toiling endlessly and struggling to catch up, and so had not made close friends at school with the exception of one girl, Hangaama, the daughter of a local businessman. She had transferred into my class from another class. She was a newcomer, too, so it was easy to strike up a friendship.

Hangaama had a photographic memory and could memorize and regurgitate verbatim, and with great ease, any of the many history lessons in our textbooks from beginning to end. This phenomenal ability to rattle off an entire lesson by heart was a skill that was much liked by our teachers who lectured in a top-down manner without interruption. To them, individual as well as *en masse* regurgitation of a lecture by the students was a measure of how well they had understood and mastered the material. I used to marvel at Hangaama's uncanny talent, although in the process her eyes would blink neurotically as she tried to remember every detail and every word in correct order. As she continued to parrot, it appeared there was an invisible hand periodically turning each page of the book with each cock of the head between blinks. Hangaama helped me with memorizing by regurgitating, as many times as I needed, all that she had memorized. What I liked about her was her kindness, sensitivity, and willingness to help me. Taking the time, she would selflessly repeat over and over again any lesson I had trouble with. She had a caring and generous heart.

Another application of memorization in our education, which was void of critical thinking, was in our vocabulary lessons. To learn Farsi vocabulary, we divided our notebook pages into three columns, entitled "word," "meaning," and "sentence," which we would memorize. Memorization was the foundation of all learning, the basis on which to build what was considered all knowledge. I opined that the following saying captured the essential flaw in this thinking, applicable to life's other false starts as well:

خشت اول چو نهد معمار کج   تا ثریا میرود دیوار کج

Khishtay awal choo nihad maymaar kaj
Taa Sorayaa mayrawad deewaar kaj

Should the first brick by the builder crookedly be laid,
To the constellation will the wall crookedly cascade

—Tabrizi

Although in school memorization and rote learning were considered paramount, coming from a family with a more progressive approach to education, I knew that this approach was not optimal. However, I realized I was not going to change the system. To summarize in one's own words was not considered a strength.

Making friends in Malalai was not easy. Other girls in my class were not as warm or friendly as Hangaama. When the twelve government cabinet ministers were appointed during the school year, we all tuned into the radio for the announcements of this big national event. My classmates did not congratulate me or even acknowledge my father's new appointment as Minister of Education. This was no insignificant news. But word had probably gotten around of my father's impressive credentials and radically progressive ideas and strides made in democratizing and modernizing the country. Although his ideas were almost always initially challenged in government circles, most were ultimately instituted, often leaving upper-level authoritarian-leaning government officials—whose daughters were my classmates— disquieted. Once, in a tête à tête with Homaira, I complained about my unfriendly classmates. She said I shouldn't worry because they were probably just jealous of who I was, my looks, or perhaps my fluent English. Hearing Homaira's reasons for their unkind behavior made dealing with these girls a little less difficult and unpleasant.

In Kabul, everybody recognized everybody and certainly everyone knew of the cabinet ministers and their families. My classmates knew exactly who I was even though I was being ignored. The snubbing—be it of royal family members and their affiliates who were in my class, or teachers who were at the opposite end of the political spectrum, with budding leftist penchants—was quite obvious. However, I was never as overtly bullied in Afghanistan as I would be in boarding school. The day after my father's name was announced, Hangaama came to me with a warm smile and gave me a hug. I was grateful for my loyal friend.

After family loyalty, learning was at the core of our family values. When I was growing up, education dominated my whole life and *raison d'*être. With two highly educated parents, our access to knowledge was a gift, and we were deeply committed to school and our studies. Having completed his undergraduate and graduate studies at the University of Chicago, my father became an avant-garde trailblazer for progressive education in Afghanistan. One of a few in his time to be selected to study abroad, upon return, he was at the vanguard of not only expanding education for young Afghans throughout the country but also for exploring, implementing, and championing novel ideas in his many pilot schools and in his other government-related jobs. Possessing a deep understanding of his people, and a master at bringing together Afghans of diverse backgrounds to effect positive change, my father was, to me, the embodiment of enlightened thinking.

During grammar school, after our usual full-time Afghan school day, my younger siblings and I were bused to the local American Academy to study an English curriculum. One day, we were given a homework assignment that I found overwhelmingly difficult. My father helped us tackle it, making the time to sit down with me and my younger siblings as we drank tea and speedily shelled and devoured delicious roasted pine nuts. We brainstormed ideas before excitedly spewing out the actual words as we collectively composed a poem. To help us with this assignment and generate results, my father simply asked questions, finessing out of us the following indelible ending to our constructed poem for English class. A description of the Afghan spirit and lines he elicited and we composed were,

> Dauntless and brave
> Fearful of nothing
> Children of the mountains
> Victory we claim.

This description of spirit, which I would later learn in my Afghan high school, has also been the subject of the great Farsi poets and has haunted any and all foreign adversaries and invaders of the nation. These simple lines were aligned with an intrinsic national pride and identity, which is associated with immense self-respect, valor, and bravery against all intruders, which Afghans have exhibited throughout history. Emanating from profound nationalistic pride and the warrior mentality, akin to a Spartacus or Braveheart, the poet foretells what awaits anyone who may transgress an Afghan:

گر ندانی غیرت افغانی ام   چون به میدان آمدی میدانی ام

Gar nadaanee ghairatay Afghaanee am
Choon ba maidaan aamadee maydaanee am

If ever my Afghan valor you should not comprehend
Whereupon entering the battlefield, you will come to understand

—Abdulali Mustaghny

When I was an adolescent, my father recited a more sophisticated graphic description of battle in a poem whose exciting alliteration, rhythm, rhyme, and all-round anticipation and drama of actual battle, transported me to the awesome terror of real wars, waged long ago:

ز سم ستوران در آن پهن دشت   زمین شش شد و آسمان گشت هشت

به روز نبرد آن یل ارجمند   به شمشیر و گرز و به تیغ و کمند

درید و برید و شکست و ببست   یلان را سر و سینه و پا و دست

Zi sumay sutooraan dar aan pahan dasht
Zameen shash shud o aasmaan gasht hasht
Ba rozay nabard aan yalay arjomand
Ba shamshayr o gurz o ba teegh o kamand
Dareed o bureed o shikast o bibast
Yalaan raa sar o seena o paa o dast

60

Below the rumbling hooves of horses in that vast ongoing desert dust
Earth's layers dwindled to six, whilst heaven's soared to level eight
On the day of battle, the most valiant and venerable
With swords, blades, clubs and lassos, well-armed,
Gored, gashed, bludgeoned and entangled
As the enemy's heads, breasts, legs and arms, they mangled

—Firdowsi

A similar depiction of battles I later encountered was the juxtaposition of words in a song from the 1960s production of Camelot: "Bash and thrash him. Smash and mash him. Give him trouble. He will be rubble. Pierce right through him. Barbecue him." Although I thought the words of this song were fairly witty, I did not come away with quite the same forceful impact as I derived from the Farsi poem.

7. Jashin

Thoughts of the Farsi war poem and the movie *Camelot* made me remember the Afghan celebration, Jashin. It was in line with a very keen sense of bravery in war and with great national pride that Afghans were victorious in defeating the British three different times in their expansionist attempts. A British general named McNaughton, who was defeated in one of the final battles, is mocked even today by children learning about Afghan-British history. With jeers, they imitate him as limping and slinking shamefully, from Afghanistan all the way back to British India.

The ousting of the British from Afghanistan was commemorated in a national celebration called Jashin. It was one of the most cherished—and fun—annual events in the country. This victory celebration was full of merrymaking that lasted for ten days. Not only was Jashin a complete break from all studying, but it was filled with novel activities that were exhilarating. The place to be for this grand festival was Kabul. As the capital, it had the most lights and fanfare in the entire country. Normally, electricity in Afghanistan was scarce, but during the ten days of Jashin, there was no scarcity of power. The whole city, at least to my young eyes, was brilliantly ablaze with colorful lights lining all the streets and buildings. It was a period of rich exposure to various cultures and international exhibitions, with an array of music and singing, dances, and acrobatic performances from leading Soviet, Chinese, Pakistani, Indian, and Iranian artists, as well as indigenous Afghans. It was a magnificent mélange of different peoples, art, cuisine, and cultures of all kinds in wonderful settings, both indoors and outside, under huge tents in various venues referred to as camps, each one named after one of the twelve ministries as well as one for the king.

To this day, I have never seen quite the likes of the expert Chinese acrobats whose tricks never ceased to amaze me. In one performance, with their backs on the floor, they would spin in the air, between their toes, entire large upside-down tables, gently kicking and passing them down an assembly line across and around a stage of other spinners who would do the same. The food in the camps was plentiful and as we devoured the mouth-watering kebabs, we'd enjoy being serenaded by small groups of musicians, usually sitting cross-legged on bright, plush scarlet Afghan carpets with the popular elephant-foot pattern.

The entertainers were well-known Afghan masters such as Saraahang, Amaahang, Shaidaa, Rahim Bakhsh, and others, whose music was heavily influenced by the classical *ragas* of masters of the subcontinent such as Salaamatali and Nizaakatali as well as famous singers of *ghazals* or lyrical poems from Pakistan and India. Very adeptly, these singers could manipulate their voices in undulating fashion, which had a mesmerizing effect on audiences and served as a great backdrop to the magical, mystical evening festivities. Occasionally, adults were privy to concerts by the likes of Ravi Shankar.

One of the highlights of the ten nights was a magnificent firework display, whose closest and best vantage point was from the venue of the king and his entourage. However, I found the other venues to be more relaxed, with less pomp and ceremony and, therefore, more enjoyable.

The other nights were devoted to mirth and merrymaking with friends, family, and extended family, either at home, in and around the various venues, or at any of the many performances. The toughest decision was narrowing down the vast number of options available, coming to a consensus, and finally mapping out our itinerary. Then we kids would all squeeze into one of our cars—a Russian jeep or Chevrolet, whichever our parents could spare. With an older cousin at the helm, and of course, no seatbelts for safety, we piled on laps, one on top of another. In the process, skirts got caught up in doors, tied up in legs, or were ripped by shoes and heels, but none of this prevented us from laughing hysterically as we barreled out of the driveway in pursuit of all the fun ahead! The first stop, and big treat, was a bottle of Coca-Cola for each of us from the Khyber restaurant. Sometimes, we even disobeyed Mom's rule and bought a soda from a local store that had a marble at the top of the bottle. We'd push down the marble and the fizz would squirt out as we frantically licked, trying to stop the overflow. This drink was even better than the fancy Coke with pop-off tops.

Another exciting event was viewing a Buzkashi game, performed in the main Kabul stadium. It's similar to polo although less civil than the British game. We always sat in what we called the *loge*, a covered balcony area a few rows away from the king and other dignitaries. Although we had a great vantage point, the game was sometimes hard to follow, but always exciting. It was difficult to differentiate the fierce participants on each team because of all the commotion and no real difference in the team uniforms.

The two teams would start out on horses, in a massive crowded cluster of entangled bodies, whipping one another and creating great clouds of dust as they struggled frantically. Players would dip down from their horse, often with only one foot secured in a stirrup, and try to grab and pick up off the ground the carcass of a goat. The goat was like a prized ball and the focal point of the game. Before the game, the dead goat had gone through a treatment that made it heavy and prepared it for the durability necessary to be yanked and tossed around in the rough game without being torn to shreds.

After fighting in the cluster of horses and bodies for what seemed like an eternity to us, one horseman would finally break away, clenching his whip like a bit in his teeth while holding the horse's reins with one hand and firmly gripping the goat with the other. He would carry on thus, the goat dangling, bobbing up and down and thrashing the side of his horse which was in full gallop, all the while being relentlessly pursued by the other players. This chase continued along a prescribed route all the way to a designated area where he then would drop the goat next to his team's flag. If he succeeded, he would score a hard-earned goal.

Although there must have been rules that governed this game, it seemed to us that there were no limits or rules. There were certainly no outside referees as in soccer or tennis. We watched with a mixture of horror and awe these uncommon behaviors which were so alien to us.

We thought Buzkashi was fun to watch in Kabul, but the best game I ever saw was up in the province of Takhaar, located in the northern region of the country where the game originated. There, it was held in a vast open field instead of the more confining stadium in Kabul. We were special guests of the governor and enjoyed the magnificent full gallop of horses running wild and free through the expansive space. I will never forget the excitement of this special experience.

The game ended with a shocking finale. After the final goal was scored, one of the players on the winning team trotted over to salute my father. As he did so, he dipped down, and with great ease picked up my nine-year-old brother with one hand, plopping him down securely in front of him on the horse. It was as though my brother was the goat we'd been seeing tossed around in the game. In a flash, the horseman galloped off into the distance. I could see my horrified mother gasping in disbelief. Later, to our great relief, my brother, totally exhilarated by the experience, was returned to us safe and sound, wanting more.

Buzkashi game in Northern Afghanistan

Thor returns after a ride with a *chaapandaaz* (Buzkashi player).

I am sitting on the couch (2nd from left) with Mom and her friends during Jashin festivities in Kabul

8. Shangri-la

During my US-bound flight, the further I traveled from Afghanistan, the more my thoughts flashed back to my early childhood in Lashkargah. As a young girl, I always smiled, even if I was experiencing difficulties. Whether the smile was truly radiant or a mere glint of a smile, there was a smile nonetheless.

A remarkable trait of most Afghans is the seemingly effortless ability to smile and also laugh, even amidst tragic circumstances. On the last stretch of my journey, I remembered fondly the tranquility of childhood which automatically brought a bittersweet smile to my face as I recalled an entreaty that reconciles internal and external contradictory manifestations. Always impressed by the admirable grace of people under extreme conditions of duress, my father would often comment,

دلا به باغ برو مشرب از انار آموز   که موج خون به دل و خنده در دهن دارد

Dilaa ba baagh birow mashrab az anaar aamoze
Ki mowjay khoon ba dil o khanda dar dahan daarad

Oh beloved, visit the orchard to learn the pomegranate's disposition
It churns waves of blood within the heart while beaming a smile in apparition

—Rumi

En route to New York, I thought about this couplet and remembered with a nostalgic smile all the places of my early childhood before

Kabul when my father was governor of Helmand Province or "Wilaayatay Waadee Helmand," a vast arid region of mostly barren desert that he and his team of Afghans and Americans were trying to develop through multiple engineering projects and irrigation feats with the help of USAID. The project and contract was huge, involving the combined efforts of many American, international, and Afghan engineers, all working together with my father to make the province prosper. My siblings and I grew up with the families of these workers in a small town called Lashkargah, the capital of Helmand province. Lashkargah was several hours at a distance from, and thus in sharp contrast to the major city, Kandahar.

Being far away from Kandahar allowed for a more autonomous and freer lifestyle for us in Lashkargah, which was more in tune with my parent's liberal values. Adults set their own standards for how to live. Women and girls within the confines of our town did not wear the *chaadaree*, the head and face covering and body shroud that was still required in the far stricter and more conservative provinces, including Kabul. Being tucked away in the remote desert of southern Afghanistan, we fell outside of the boundaries of the pervasive surveillance, scrutiny, and dictates of the central government.

There were no schools yet in Lashkargah, so these had to be established in both American and Afghan systems by drawing on the various skills and talents of adults in the community. Wherever there were gaps in the American system, my older siblings were home-schooled with supplementary programs and materials that were developed by the University of Chicago.

What I enjoyed most about school was recess when I could use my above average height to full advantage in games of tetherball as I often managed to whip the ball, sending it twirling around the post before others could reach it. The ego-boost of each full 360-degree twirl was exhilarating. I also loved to play soccer because I was sure that my captain, Linda Logan, to whom I was devoted, would choose me as her goalie. I took this position very seriously and loved receiving her praises when I would faithfully and selflessly block oncoming goals with my bare thighs, since I usually wore a skirt to school. The redder my thighs from impact, the more pleased I'd be, knowing I'd shown my commitment and loyalty to the captain and the team. Another game, more in the realm of imagination, was when we'd prance around pretending to be *gaadees*, and in pairs we would roleplay the horses and their drivers holding imaginary reins, as we'd gallop around the schoolyard.

My early years proved the universal truism that "kids will be kids." Even though studying was a big part of our lives, the full gravity and importance of school came to me later in Kabul. In Lashkargah, the days were more frivolous and often slow and lazy because of the ever-present extreme, and often debilitating, dry heat. Although there was no humidity, the scorching temperatures were draining. We lived in the governor's mansion which was very large with many rooms. The walls of the mansion were thick and the ceilings high, but it was still hot in the rooms since there was no air conditioning. Instead, to relieve us of the extreme heat, the house had several swamp or desert coolers on each of the floors.

For fun, we would jump up and down with delight for hours on the mattresses of our beds, which sat on metal springs that propelled us high up in the air. This trampoline-like activity required much energy, causing us to sweat profusely, but we would continue, going higher and higher until we literally nearly hit our heads on the ceiling. Afterwards, we would take a cold shower, standing upside down in the stall as the water flowed over our bodies, cooling us down. My older sister discovered another option for relief from the sweltering heat. Each of us followed her rather dangerous example by taking turns crawling inside the chamber that housed the swamp cooler in our bedroom. Sitting there, crouched up and being extra careful not to get our hair or clothes caught up in the whirling fan blades, not only did we enjoy the full force of cool air but we also found the whirring sound relaxing.

The activities each day were nonstop. For the children, this entailed endless hours of indiscriminately jumping over fences whose barriers we transgressed without a care. Then we'd climb trees on the other side that we thought all belonged to us. While balancing our limbs on branches, we would pick, and then gorge on, the limitless quantity of delicious, fresh, ripe mulberries, to which we felt entitled. After eating to our hearts' content, with bellies full, we'd ride our bikes round and round the blocks. Once, my brother rode with such fervor that his bike rolled off a path into a swampy ditch by the river. He became entangled in his bike which had toppled on top of him and was miraculously saved from drowning by our older cousin Zalmay, who just happened to be close by. After our bike rides, with special keys we would screw on our roller skates that Mom on one of her trips to the States had purchased, and in sheer delight, we tore around our homes on the newly formed concrete sidewalks which had recently been constructed, often crashing on hairpin turns. Unsurprisingly, there were many scabs and bruises, but to our parent's chagrin, these never stopped us.

There were a few mishaps for me in Lashkargah although these never diminished my love for my hometown. Once, our Soviet jeep came to a screeching halt, causing me to fly forward and break my nose on the bar of the seat in front of me. Although I was only two years old when it happened, the excruciating pain from the impact is still unforgettable. An American doctor staunched the blood and expertly stitched me up so that the scar formed is barely visible. Another time, I got a nose bleed that wouldn't stop. Again, an American doctor came to the rescue. He laid me across the cool bathroom floor and blocked the affected nostril with his finger in such a way that the flow stopped.

One year, I contracted malaria. My long-lasting low-grade fever was exacerbated by the ever-present intense heat. Having little energy, I dragged myself around, unhappy that I couldn't play like other children. I dreaded the regular trips to an American doctor far away for my treatment. On each visit, I was obliged to swallow the dreadfully bitter doses of quinine. To tolerate my regimen, I would desperately try to escape by imagining some sort of activity to look forward to.

This much desired break would be the privilege of dunking myself and swimming for several hours in the outdoor community swimming pool. None of us could wait for this luxurious relief from the perpetual heat. We were usually so excited that we couldn't sleep and often faked the daily nap we were supposed to take prior to heading out for this anxiously awaited daily high point. A swimming pool was a radical novelty in Afghanistan and involved what would have been considered by high authorities to be the brazen practice of nudity since much of our bodies were exposed by the swimsuits we wore. Somehow though, with our physical distance from the rest of humanity, we were out of the surveillance range of the ogres in positions of authority and were thus left alone in our blissful little cocoon that many referred to simply as "Lash." Whatever obstacles that might have arisen were handled by my father who was experienced, methodical, persuasive, and most often successful in affecting change.

The layout of buildings in our section of town was simple. The community pool, tennis courts, governor's mansion, other homes, and the clubhouse for guests were all located in one line on the same street. The large, wide Helmand Valley River paralleled these and ran gushing beside them. Our school was across the street, a few doors down. The community pool and its surroundings were a great venue for kids and adults alike. After the kids played there all afternoon, sometimes at night, the area was aglow with lights when used by adults for evening parties and socializing. On the other side, across the river, was a strip of land that the Americans named "Pig Island," known for its wild boars. Adults used to take aim and hunt them from where we lived across the wide river. A couple of times, the king visited for hunting, too. Having lived extensively in France, he and his entourage were favorably impressed by the completely novel, modern utopian haven in Lashkargah and approved of the amalgam of cultures that existed there as well as the fostering of a wonderful cooperative *esprit de corps* of its inhabitants. Very familiar with American culture and being an expert in understanding the nuances and subtleties of his own people, my father managed to navigate each culture and bridge both and was able to establish close personal and professional relations with all his colleagues, whether Afghan or American. He served as an effective facilitator wherever necessary and fostered a harmonious work environment among all of those same coworkers.

At the governor's mansion there were beautiful scenes of adult life that I observed from a distance, sitting at the large open window of the master bedroom on the second floor, which overlooked the sprawling lawn. Sometimes, my parents entertained their Afghan and American colleagues there, serenading them in private outdoor concerts featuring local and national musicians. I used to watch with fascination as daylight slowly dimmed and the desert temperature dropped. There on the lawn, beside a blooming garden and bright multicolored palate of wild roses, geraniums, petunias, sweet peas, and snapdragons, the adults would all sit and relax under light wraps, enjoying the soft, cool summer breezes.

As they sipped cup after cup of hot cardamom-flavored tea, they would listen to the strains of authentic Afghan music slowly rising in the air. Sitting a short distance in front of them, a professional singer or *ustaad* would begin to perform slowly, skillfully manipulating his voice in typical *aalaabs*, or wordless, intricate long-winded up-and-down scales. Gradually, in his repertoire, he would introduce touching lyrics which were punctuated subsequently with mesmerizing refrains replete with mind-blowing poetry of the likes of Baydil and Rumi. The *ustaad* singer was accompanied throughout by a melodious harmonium evoking liltingly complementary chords. The harmonium and singer were accompanied by the softly tapped pair of drums of one *tabla chi*—a drummer, whose fingers moved rapidly and then fluttered so skillfully that they became invisible. Musicians sat only a few yards away from the guests. The voice of the singer and his words were always crystal clear and never drowned out by accompanying music. Because of the small gathering and peaceful surroundings of utter quiet, loudspeakers were not needed.

With the magnificent unobstructed view and backdrop of a brilliant orange- and red-streaked sky and a sun like a giant desert fireball setting beyond the river below, it was a picturesque, magical scene of incomparable beauty and serenity. As I sat upstairs watching, I welled up with immense pride at my parents' ability to bring people of so many diverse backgrounds together to enjoy such rich cultural experiences.

Throughout my life, music has filled voids and consoled me. Listening to it has been my favorite pastime and a great source for educating myself, not only about Afghanistan but about the world beyond. Occasionally, our parents took us to a little town, Chaanjeer, where along with other Americans we had the rare pleasure of watching carefully selected movies such as Lucille Ball comedies, *My Fair Lady*, *Gigi*, and *Singing in the Rain*. It was in seeing these enchanting productions that my fascination and love for words was born. I relished the storylines of each movie and memorized the lyrics of all the musicals.

I am the third of five children who, while growing up, was considered too young to join my older siblings in their activities and lessons in knitting, ballet, drama, water ballet, and the like. Since I was not happy to be relegated to the company of my younger siblings, I found music from all parts of the world and all eras to be an enjoyable outlet and escape. I spent many hours alone, playing records over and over on our gramophone until I memorized from my parents' classical collection the themes of pieces by Rachmaninoff, Grieg, Chopin, Debussy, Liszt, Wagner, and Tchaikovsky. Treasuring the collection of these records, I was very careful when lifting and lowering the needle on the gramophone to avoid scratching and damaging them. The cherished records were both large and small, either 33's or 78's. My father was an ardent lover of music as well. Some of his Eastern favorites were the duets of Lata Mangeshkar and Rafi, and his favorite of all was Saigal, whose voice he could imitate perfectly. Often in the mornings, I could hear him singing through the walls as he was shaving for work; the likeness of his voice to Saigal's was uncanny.

When my precocious older sister, Rona, was around eleven or twelve, she was allowed to have parties with her age group in the gardens at the governor's mansion, just as my parents did. I envied that she had this privilege, and of course, I was too young to attend or have a party of my own. I would watch these special social events with keen interest from the same bedroom window that I watched my parents' parties.

During a two-week period, Rona was engrossed in reading *Gone with the Wind*, and while she and my mother discussed the book, I would sometimes eavesdrop. As I listened, I imagined my sister as a "Scarlett" in a back-and-forth with a person whose name I had seen written on the page but could not pronounce. Trying to steal some of my mother's undivided attention during these sessions, and probably much to my sister's irritation, I went around the house chirping my mispronounced version of his name: "Re-het Bootler! Re-het Bootler!"

One of Rona's closest friends was Elaine Simonson—a slightly older, beautiful platinum blonde American girl. She was very glamorous and wore all the latest styles. I remember seeing her once in a fancy dress, which had a hoop skirt that didn't budge but stuck out and kept its starched, rigid circular shape from her waist all the way around her lower body, even when she moved. Watching the party unfold, I gazed at Elaine's every fluid hand, arm, and upper torso move and her very alluring, graceful glides which caused the skirt to gently bob up and down. As I watched, I dreamily looked forward to a time when I, too, might be old enough to host such a grand soirée and could wear a hoop skirt just like the one I had seen and admired on Elaine.

On Halloween and Christmas holidays, we were finally all lumped together, regardless of age. We enjoyed spending time with our American friends and made creative costumes which we would trick or treat in. Once, I was supposed to be a ballerina, although I'm not sure how sticking a nylon stocking over the hair on my head, which was a bit of a stretch, turned me into one. The best part, of course, were all the chocolates and candy we got from American homes, whose pantries were well-stocked with such treats from the US commissary.

At Christmas time, we'd partake in caroling or watch the older kids perform *A Christmas Carol* in the staff house, the central building for business and social affairs of primarily the American personnel in Lashkargah. For us, the emphasis was on having fun and participating in the activities of our community and not about practicing concepts in piety or religion.

A few times my father would take us to nearby Kandahar to celebrate the Afghan New Year known as *Now Roz* on March 20. Kandahar was the closest, biggest city in the south where we would get an authentic taste of national traditions and celebrations. During these visits, we'd watch riveting performances of the national dance, called the *Atan*. Although many Afghans perform it, the most expert dancers were the men in Kandahar. I was born in a hospital located in Kandahar, so I felt particularly proud of these Kandahari dancers. They are typically extremely attractive, well built, tall, and broad-shouldered with small waists and shoulder-length, jet-black hair.

Performing the *Atan*, the dancers would start out on a field in a circle, barefoot, all dressed in national costume, a white *payraan* (flowing shirt), a *tunbaan* (baggy pantaloons), and a *waaskat*, (an ornate red velvet vest outlined with thick, shimmering gold strips sewn onto it, forming special designs as accents). One of the dancers held a huge drum strapped to both his neck and back, and he began banging it slowly but loudly on both sides, with his hand-held drum sticks. The dancers took steps following his lead and continued to pick up speed, keeping in time with the drummer. As the beat got faster and louder, the dancers became more and more frenetic, hopping up high, kicking up the dirt, twisting and turning in the air, and making full 360-degree turns while jerking their heads left and right, sending their black hair flying. Every so often to continue the frenzy, they would dip and squat down all the way to the ground, springing back up on one foot to a standing position while waving a small handkerchief in the air. I always marveled at their great agility, speed, and sustained gracefulness.

Another spectacle in Kandahar during the *Now Roz* celebrations was *Naiza Baazee,* which was a more civilized version of what the medieval knights in Europe practiced. In this sport in Europe, men on horses used the same skill, precision, and accuracy of spearing a human opponent, but in *Naiza Baazee,* they would lean and bend down on the side of the horse while aiming for and spearing a peg that had been embedded in the ground. Then they would hold the speared peg up high for the whole crowd to see and applaud.

Fridays were our days off from work and school. My siblings and I would pile into the car for long drives with my dad who would monitor the progress of landmark infrastructure sites throughout the Helmand Valley that he and his team were working so hard to build. Never in my wildest dreams did I ever imagine that the towns of Lashkargah, Chaanjeer, Maarja, and Girishk would make world headlines in the twenty-first century and become war zones in the longest war ever waged by the US.

A few times, my father took us to Kajakai, which had a huge hydroelectric-power dam, built by the US Morrison-Knudsen company. This trip took several days. Because of the scarcity of water in the Helmand Valley, going to Kajakai with Dad, his team of engineers, and their families was a rare and cherished treat. Since Afghanistan is a landlocked country, I had never seen so much water in one place as in Kajakai. The dam was one of the biggest projects ever to be undertaken in Afghanistan and was one of the greatest feats in engineering, using the combined efforts of, among others, American, Italian, and Filipino experts. Of course, I didn't know how it worked, but I loved going there to see and experience the torrent of water flowing over the dam. As we approached Kajakai, I'd stick my head out of the car window with eager anticipation to catch a brief glimpse of the mighty flow of water spewing out of the spillway. Swimming in those open waters was quite a bit more thrilling than swimming in our little pool in Lashkargah. To relax, the adult men fished, and we would eat their fresh catch at night. What a delicious treat it was! We'd all sit on the lawn of our bungalow for dinner, my only wish being that there could be fewer bones so that I could gobble it down faster.

The rich, creamy ice cream I could eat to my heart's content in the American commissary or mess hall was another high point of Kajakai.

For me, and many who lived there, Lashkargah was a blissful Utopia—a perfect, peaceful little paradise that would never again be approximated, let alone repeated, in our lifetime. Growing up in a household of two loving parents, living in a connected community of friendly American and Afghan families, all socializing, going to school, and working harmoniously side by side, I felt the greatest sense of belonging, tranquility, and safety.

On the plane ride to New York, these childhood memories added to my homesickness. A song echoing my feelings rang in my head. It was made popular by my cousin Ahmad Zahir, considered to be the Afghan Elvis and a top vocalist of the time and to this day:

نشاط عمر به پایان رسید و افسوس   بهار جوانی ام رفت و ا افسوس
سوی آسمانها رفت و افسوس   خوشی ام همچو عقاب کرده پرواز

Bahaaray jawaanee am raft o afsos
Nishaatay umur ba paa- een raseed o afsos
Khushee am hamchoo uqaab karda parwaaz
Soy aasmaanhaa raft o afsos

The springtime of youth has gone, alas!
Life's joyfulness has reached its nadir, alas!
My happiness, 'twas like an eagle that took flight
Towards the skies it departed, oh alas!

Like notes floating from a distant reed in a melancholy tune, memories of leaving my homeland summoned up an iconic and celebrated poem:

از جدایی ها شکایت میکند   بشنو از نی چون حکایت میکند

از نفیرم مرد و زن نالیده اند   کز نیستان تا مرا ببریدند

Bishnow az nai choon hikaayat maykunad

Az judaa-eehaa shikaayat maykunad

Kaz naistaan taa maraa bibreedand

Az nafeeram mard o zan naaleeda and

Listen to the reed that tells a story

Of panged separations, it blares forlornly

From my patch in the field when plucked and banished

For my lamentations, men and women weep with anguish

—Rumi

My thoughts drifted again to the pomegranate, so prevalent in Afghan culture. It plays a big part both in everyday life and metaphorically in Farsi poetry where many comparisons between this fruit and humans have been made. For centuries, it has been alluded to when depicting human difficulty and turmoil. In times of trouble, whether mildly discouraging, disappointing, difficult, or even calamitous, poets have conjured the image of a pomegranate. Gazing closely into this fruit, one can see the internal magenta, blood-like waves of juice about to be unleashed from within. The small protrusion of a mouth, breaking open into a smile on its crimson skin belies the contradiction within. One is apprised at once of a constructive way to cope with adversity: laugh outwardly, as does the pomegranate, even though internally one's heart is bleeding.

Of course, during everyday life in Lashkargah, there was a much more tangible way to enjoy a pomegranate's rich complexity, unaccompanied by any analysis. By going to the orchard and smashing the fruit or by breaking it open and crushing the many kernels, I released its inner sweet, exquisite taste. Once I opened my thermos under the scorching midday Helmand desert sun, there were no seeds or any bitterness to worry about and no labor of crushing, squeezing, or purifying; what remained was a home-prepared, plentiful supply of delectable, sweet juice to drink. The soothing cool liquid trickled out of the thermos into my mouth and flowed down my parched throat—the ultimate relief from the extreme, dry heat. What an effortless way this was to celebrate life's simplest of pleasures! Referring to supreme excellence, this poet has expressed perfectly the sentiments I treasure about my birthplace:

اگر بهشت به روی زمین است   همین است و همین است و همین است

Agar bihisht ba rooy zameen ast
Hameen ast o hameen ast o hameen ast!

If paradise would appear on the face of earth
It is this, this is it, this has to be it!

Family portrait in my hometown, Lashkargah: (front row:) Mom, Thor, Trina, Dad, Nina. (back row:) Rona, Marya.

II. Embarkment

1. Bewildering Encounters

An intercom announcement abruptly brought me back down to earth. We were nearing the end of the Atlantic Ocean. Shortly, we would be landing in New York. I was glued to my window, peering out in anticipation of spotting water and giant waves. The sublime, enchanted days of childhood began to fade as my East-to-West odyssey continued. My focus shifted from the past to solving more urgent, present-moment challenges. Upon disembarking from the plane in New York, I was jolted by the huge, impersonal, and overwhelming entity, that is, John F. Kennedy International Airport. To help me feel less intimidated, I remembered my father's counsel:

مرد باید که هراسان نشود   مشکلی نیست که آسان نشود

Mard baayad kay hiraasaan nashawad
Mushkilay nayst ki aasaan nashawad

One need not be afraid
There is no difficulty that cannot be allayed

—Abdul Haamid Baluch

Imbued with a sort of blind confidence, I kept my wits about me remembering what Afghans say when faced with any hurdle:

کمر را بسته کن و آستین ها را بر بزن

Kamar raa basta kun o aasteenhaa raa bar bizan

Tie your waist tightly, and roll up your sleeves

Performing both of these mentally, I quickly joined forces with my siblings as we strategized our next moves. One very important piece of advice our father drummed into us was never to be afraid to ask questions, no matter how many or how dumb they seemed to us. After many inquiries and scads of coins which we frantically shoved into the coin-operated pay phone, we dialed area codes and long number sequences, listening to unfamiliar dial tones. By some miracle, after many tries, we managed to get through to Rosanne Klass—a long-time, good friend of our parents and our only American contact. "Aunt" Rosanne had been instrumental as a liaison for our family in the US. Mom and Dad had asked her to help in selecting a short list of the best US boarding schools for boys and girls. She was very thorough in her research and provided the names of top schools that were in geographic proximity to one another. Among these, Mom chose Emma Willard because of its outstanding reputation. After we landed in New York, we were eager to meet up with Aunt Rosanne and looked forward to feeling a bit more secure in her presence. We took several buses and trains out of the complicated entanglement of Kennedy airport, scrambling to find seats in what felt like a competitive dog-eat-dog situation.

Finally, we found our way to our friend's apartment in Manhattan. We stayed with her for several days and were subjected to urgent lectures in her two-day crash course on living in and getting around America. We listened intently to her well-intended but seemingly never-ending advice. She also fed us lots of her favorite New York recipe, *chili con carne*, which was quite tasty.

Before departing Kabul, my parents gave each of us $200 in cash, tucked in separate envelopes, with which to make our way to our respective schools. This was a lot by Afghan standards, but with the exchange rate of 80 Afghanis to the dollar, it did not amount to much money in America. My father probably knew this as he sent us off with a confession:

چه کند بینوا همین دارد   برگ سبز است تحفهٔ درویش

Bargay sabz ast tohfay darwaysh
Chi kunad baynawaa hameen daarad

A green leaf is the dervish's gift
Poor voiceless soul, 'tis all he has

However, my father had very responsibly calculated that, with his dependable contacts along the way, this amount would be sufficient to get us to our schools. Once in school, with our scholarships, we would thankfully not need to worry about expenses.

On one occasion, I left Aunt Rosanne's New York City apartment and ventured out into Manhattan to see some of the big city. I was impressed by all the glass and concrete skyscrapers on West 72nd Street and crowds of people everywhere. All of this was like nothing I had ever seen before. It was quite overwhelming, and I felt as insignificant as an ant. I dared not venture far for fear of getting lost. I knew, however, that much could be discovered even when one was lost, since

سیل هم سیل ، سرگردانی هم سیل

Sail ham sail,
Sar gardaany ham sail

Sightseeing is sightseeing
Being lost is also sightseeing

I felt a mixture of apprehension and excitement. However, the need to explore, to leverage my time in New York, won. With the idea, "Seek and ye shall find," floating in my head, I walked south from her apartment where I found a small store. I decided to buy a few items of clothing to help me fit in when I got to the school. I knew there would be many adjustments to make and thought it was important to eliminate awkward first impressions. Wanting to blend in made me think of "When in Rome do as the Romans do," and its Farsi equivalent:

خواهی نشوی رسوا، همرنگ جماعت باش

Khwaahee nashawee ruswaa,
Hamrangay jamaa-at baash

Should you not want to live in infamy
Be in kind with society

I bought a pair of jeans and an oversized men's white-and-blue-striped shirt. The look, I thought was simple and understated like a hippy, which I gathered was the current style. I was careful not to overspend as I still had a few days before getting to school and recalled the admonition,

به حال آن کس باید گریست   که دخلش بود نوزده و خرچش بیست

Ba haalay aankas baayad gireest
Ki dakhlash bouad nuzda wa kharchash beest

For the predicament of that person one ought to cry
Whose income is nineteen and expenses twenty.

After a couple of days, we bade goodbye to Aunt Rosanne and embarked on the journey to our schools in Vermont, Troy and Rochester, New York, and New Hampshire (Middlebury College, Emma Willard, University of Rochester, and Phillips Exeter Academy, respectively). In my case, this entailed taking a train in Manhattan to a bus for Albany and another bus to Troy, then a taxi to Pawling Avenue and Emma Willard School, my final destination. Saying goodbye to my siblings at Penn Station in New York was not as difficult as I had imagined it might be. By then, I had already bid my most solemn goodbyes and I was eager to get to my final destination of this long journey.

When I arrived in Troy, the sky was overcast. Troy was much smaller than New York City, and a welcome respite from the overwhelming hustle and bustle of the earlier big metropolis. I found a taxi, and the driver engaged in small talk, asking me where I had come from. I proudly exclaimed, "Afghanistan!" and then he asked me if that was in Africa.

I said, "No, Asia." I was a bit surprised by his ignorance but chalked it up to his lack of education. Little did I know how many educated people of the time hadn't a clue where Afghanistan was either. In fact, some had even asked friends of mine where in the state of Texas it was located.

The cab driver had a tough time finding my school, and after a period of traveling in circles, we both finally spotted a small sign with the name Emma Willard School on it.

He then said, in an irritated fashion, "Well, they might as well have buried it!"

By now, I was quite excited to burst onto the scene, and with my heart beating fast, I stepped out of the cab, lifting my forty-five-pound suitcase. I had to haul it one last time from the school's iron gate through a groin-vaulted entryway which opened up to the serene green lawn of the campus. Thankfully, I no longer would have to lug this suitcase around. I had packed very carefully and efficiently. Even though my whole life's belongings had dwindled to a mere suitcase, I remembered thinking in minimalist fashion,

آنچه ما در کار داریم ، اکثرش در کار نیست

Aanchi maa dar kaar daaraym
Aksarash dar kaar nayst

That which we have in use
Mostly is of no use.

Glancing around, I noticed an empty chair in the shaded area of the vaulted entrance where I was standing with my suitcase. I decided to rest for a bit to catch my breath and so plopped down in the chair. My eyes carried me across the beautiful, sprawling, impeccably manicured, velvety lawns of the campus all the way to the high imposing Gothic buildings which bordered them. Although impressively large, they were somewhat intimidating.

"So, this is it." I sighed. "Finally, I have arrived."

It was the end of a long day, and I was tired. I wondered where to go next. I looked up again at the scene before me. *Give it some time*, I thought. *I'll get used to it.*

Biding my time, I repeated to myself some comforting words of respite:

شب در میان، خدا مهربان

Shab dar meeyaan
Khudaa mihrabaan

A night betwixt and between
Whereupon God's kindness will intervene

After waiting at the entrance to the campus, I was met and shown to my room by one of the upperclassmen, known as a "big sister." She was formal but nice. It was good to have the long journey behind me. After I climbed up a long, winding staircase with her, I flung the big wheel-less suitcase I had lugged around for days onto the floor of my room. I had few belongings and smiled as I was reminded of the anti-materialism story about the character of a famous homeless vagabond named *Baalol* who slept outside under a tree, his few possessions bunched up as a pillow under his head, and holding in one hand a small receptacle for loose change. He was praised for his minimalism, and it is said he was so virtuous that he went straight to heaven after exclaiming,

بالول ! یک کشکول

Baalol! Yak kashkol

Baalol owns but one small bowl!

91

With my tightly packed possessions in a small suitcase, a life-long, cumbersome and never-ending cycle of collecting things began. Keeping rather than throwing away items is more the habit, probably the result of growing up in a mostly "have-not" Afghan society. My tendency to collect rather than discard possessions is sarcastically decried by the philosophically minimalist, seasoned poet with a penchant only for the spiritual:

گویم کلیم با تو که آنهم چسان گذشت   بد نامی حیات دو روزی نبود بیش

روزی دگر به کندن دل زین و آن گذشت   روزی به صرف بستن دل شد به این و آن

Bad naamee-ay haiaat du rozay nabood baysh
Goyam Kaleem baa too ki aan ham chissaan guzasht
Rozay ba sarfay bastanay dil shud ba een o aan
Rozay digar ba kandanay dil zeen o aan guzasht

Life's disgrace lasts a mere two days
Let me (Kaleem) tell you just how each one passes
One day is spent attaching desire unto this and that
The other, by wrenching away desire from this and that, and passing

—Kaleem

I looked around my tiny room which had a small bed and even a smaller desk and dresser. Opening a miniature door on one of the walls, I crouched under into a crawl space, which had a short rod across it, to serve as a closet. Since I was used to being neat, I knew I could keep this small room tidy and was relieved to have a space, however small, of total privacy. My room was joined to a large central one that had what I thought was a plush reception area. A couple of other small rooms were also part of the alcove. There was one common bathroom that we all shared in this wing of the dorm. Soon, I met my roommate in the larger foyer which I learned was part of her bedroom. She was always there to greet anyone passing into the adjoining smaller rooms. Although, like me, a junior, she had been at Emma Willard for a year or two. She seemed nice enough although she talked a lot. For the most part, this was good because I was shy and reserved.

In the same dorm, I soon met another girl. My first impression of her was somewhat negative, but reluctant to judge prematurely, I gave her the benefit of the doubt. As I came to know her, I became aware that she was quite self-centered and inconsiderate. She expected everybody to lend her a generous ear but rarely asked others about their lives. I marveled, however, at her streak of genius in successfully managing to rope everyone around her into paying attention. Up until this point, I had never befriended anyone like her. She was very needy, and at times I felt depleted, although my emotional drain was nowhere near the severity of her troubles. Interacting with her, I often remembered the imperative inculcated in us during Afghan elementary classes:

چو استاده ای دست افتاده گیر   ره نیک مردان آزاده گیر

Rahay nayk mardaan aazaada geer
Choo istaada- ee, dastay uftaada geer

The path of humanitarians, freely take
When standing, the hand of a fallen you should take

—Sa'adi

Endeavoring to be supportive, I felt obliged to listen, which I faithfully did. Sometimes by being accommodating, I heard alarm bells go off in my head as I remembered the cautionary alert:

غم نداری بز بخر!

Gham nadaaree buz bikhar

If you have no problems, buy a goat!

93

It became obvious that I had clearly bitten off more than I could chew with this "goat". What a troublesome situation I was in! I asked myself how this happened. Was there no one else Fate might have chosen to befriend her but me? My father had always cautioned me against extending myself beyond normal or reasonable limits. However, I could not think of an exit strategy to distance myself. The situation became increasingly uncomfortable and was beginning to feel like an irreversible "fait accompli". How lonely and inexperienced I was, coming from so far afield to this school, this dormitory and this strange social situation without any confidantes such as family. Sometimes I thought maybe I was blowing the whole problem out of proportion—making a mountain out of a molehill. Remaining tolerant but hoping for a change, I mused on the wisdom and the art of patience and deferred gratification drummed into Afghan children:

صبر تلخ است، ولیکن بر شیرین دارد

Sabir talkh ast
Wa laykin baray shireen daarad

Patience is bitter
But its outcome is sweet

The sweet reward of my patience was unforthcoming for many more months. Although I was aware of counseling in school, I didn't feel comfortable or bold enough to approach a counselor to discuss what I thought was only my very personal problem of loneliness. A culturally alien concept in Afghanistan and nonexistent in Afghan schools, counseling was a new challenge with which I would have to familiarize myself. At this point, I was very uncomfortable opening up to a stranger and pouring my heart out about my feelings.

I was undergoing severe culture shock on top of being a very shy, proud, and private person. In writing class, we were encouraged to keep a journal, but I would rather have died than have my problems and inner thoughts scrutinized by teachers and their colleagues. I stuck to non-personal matters, such as describing nature scenes in all my entries. As a result, by trying to cope "solo," a "sink or swim" behavior abounded. This survivalist expectation of foreign students, particularly me (perhaps because I spoke fluent English), permeated not only academic realms but also social ones.

With the typical reticence of a sensitive, deliberate teenager and fear of potential backlash, I was unable to muster the courage to complain to anybody to change my predicament. There seemed to be no effective system in place for anyone to become aware of how I was acclimating outside the classroom so as to create, in as subtle and easy a manner as possible, a way out for students such as I. We had an aging housemother, who seemed frail and out of touch and incapable of the bold and skillful kind of intervention and help I felt was needed. Mom and Dad were far away in Afghanistan, and it would be so comforting to talk to them but to me this situation, difficult as it was, did not warrant troubling them from more than 6,500 miles away in an aerogram they would receive two or three weeks hence. The distance between us was simply too vast to address problems or seek advice on a day-to-day basis.

So I became increasingly despondent about my living situation. Although I often blamed myself for the rut I could not seem to be able to break out of, I remained hopeful nonetheless of extricating myself by eventually meeting new people. I knew there must be a way out because recalling the following wisdom gave me a measure of optimism:

چو یک در بسته گردد صد در دیگر شود پیدا   به دیوار قفس چون رخنه ها دیدم یقینم شد

Ba diwaaray qafas choon rakhnahaa deedam yaqeenam shud
Choo yak dar basta gardad sad daray deegar shawad paidaa

Upon seeing the crevices from within a cage, convinced I became
Should one door close, one hundred others shall proclaim

I was hopeful that the door of bad luck might close and a new one might open, possibly at mealtime. But I was not aware of any co-mingling of students in the cafeteria. I thought that barging into another table setting might be considered impolite and invite exclusion or embarrassment. Consequently, at every dinner, the group I initially randomly found myself in always sat together. I felt the die was cast and change was not possible. I gazed at the clusters of girls here and there and thought of the English proverb, "birds of a feather flock together," as its Farsi equivalent popped into my head:

کند همجنس با هم جنس پرواز   کبوتر با کبوتر باز با باز

Kabootar baa kabootar, baaz baa baaz
kunad hamjins ba hamjins parwaaz

Pigeons with pigeons, hawks with hawks
Like with like together always take flight

I wondered, but never discovered, what commonalities other girls shared that caused them to stick together at dinnertime. I ruminated that I had less and less in common with those at my table. Our dinner conversations centered around some variation of three themes: complaints about the bad food, poor family relations, or some crazy crush on a teacher. I wished I could emulate those who, with bravado, are able to denounce others with confidence. But I never felt I had the right nor could I muster the nerve to object to any of these conversations. And, unfortunately I lacked the gift of being able to meaningfully throw a conversation into a relevant but completely different orbit in order to change and redirect it. This skill might have relieved me of all the nonsense. Saying some variation of "No" or implementing an elementary school lesson seemed too simplistic, hard to fathom, and even harder to execute:

یک نه و صد آسان

Yak nay o sad aasaan

One "No" enables one hundred solutions

Instead, like a mute psychoanalyst, I continued to listen to the ridicule, jokes, and boasting in conversations of this mutual admiration society, which lacked humility and any notion of:

نه آنکه عطار بگوید   عطر آن است که خود ببوید

Atir aan ast ki khud buboyad
Na aan ki ataar bigoyad

A good perfume is unto itself aromatic
It needs no bluster from the perfumer, ecstatic

One of the main topics I could not relate to was how bad the food of the school was. How divorced I was from this concept, since the food to me was amazingly varied and splendid. I marveled at the daily plentiful options of entrées, salads, drinks, and desserts—which were irresistible and lead to considerable weight gain!

97

Clearly, no one here had ever experienced even secondhand the pang of hunger evoked by the poet:

این شکم بی هنر پیچ پیچ   صبر ندارد که بسازد به هیچ

Een shikamay bay hunaray paych paych
Sabir nadaarad ki bisaazad ba haych

This unproductive stomach, always churning and cramping
Has no patience whatsoever to make do with nothing.

My initial horror turned to disgust as I witnessed enormous daily volumes of untouched food jettisoned into heaping trash bins. I wondered why the waste was not noticed, understood, acknowledged, or acted upon. There were never any signs of reproach from any quarter or appreciation for the axiom, "waste not, want not," inculcated in me since childhood. I reckoned this indifference I witnessed at dinner could only be attributed to:

هر که را پیرش چنین گمراه بود   کی مریدش را به جنت راه بود

Har kiraa peerash chuneen gumraa boowad
Kai mureedash raa ba janat raa boowad

Whosoever's master is as profoundly misguided as this
How could his following ever find a way to heavenly bliss.

Other dinner conversations centered around how the girls dreaded upcoming holiday visits with parents over parents' weekend or their cross-country vacations with their "boring" families in faraway luxury resorts such as Vail, Colorado, and the like. These dissatisfactions were alien to me. If only I could see my parents somehow, anywhere, anytime, but this was not even a remote possibility! As I continued to observe and analyze the behavior of people, I was well aware of and accepted the Islamic truism,

خلق الإنسان من التفاوت

Khalaq al insan min al tafawut

He created man with differences

Scripture

Certainly, there were titanic differences in every way imaginable between me and most Emma Willard girls, from immense financial disparities to drastic differences in educational, linguistic, and cultural backgrounds; clashing value systems; tumultuous family dynamics; and many more. At fifteen, I did not have a need for anything material and felt satisfied and blessed with what little I possessed. Perhaps my partial Greek heritage had contributed to this more rugged and disciplined Spartan outlook, extolled poetically:

الفقر فخرى

Al faqro fakhri

In poverty, I am proud

The very reason for being sent to boarding school differed between me and my fellow Emma Willardians. My force majeure,

99

having been forced out of my homeland, was quite different from other girls' compulsions, and was forlornly recounted by the poet:

ما بدین در نه پی حشمت و جاه آمده ایم   ز بد حادثه اینجا به پناه آمده ایم

Maa badeen dar na pai hashmat o jaah aamada aym
Zi baday haadisa eenjaa ba panaa aamada aym

We came to this door not to pursue dignity or fame
'Tis by ill-fortune that seeking refuge here we must claim

—Haafiz

I eventually extricated myself from my living situation, an outcome achieved after quite a considerable period of forbearance and strategizing. However, it was unfortunate and remarkable that all my sensitive, one-way attention and listening did not make a dent in conversations or behavior at dinner time in the main dining hall.

2. A Name with Meaning

Like many days during my first year, one day I fell into silent reflection. I pondered my Pashto name, Tirina, and wondered if its meaning, "a good friend," was befitting of my character. I reflected on the popular custom in Afghan culture when babies were given names that evoked positive meaning that they were expected to live up to and for which they became especially known and remembered. One never encountered names such as Sally, Nancy, Jane, or Charlie, which impute no meaning or positive attribution of character to attribute to or model as in an *ismay bay musamaa* (اسم بی مسمی)—"a name with no meaning."

I repeated aloud the other axiom, *ismay baa musamaa* (اسم با مسمی)—"a name with meaning." But there seemed to be a misalignment between my name and me because as of yet, I had made no deep friendships. My thoughts drifted to my old friend, Hangaama, and I applied the same linguistic axiom of loaded meaning to her name.

"Hangaama," I repeated her name to myself softly.

"Hangaam," I murmured the root word in her name, which means "a time."

"Hangaama," I whispered her full name out loud again. I looked up and peered into the distance, taking a deep breath but seeing nothing. I had a keen sense of dread that Hangaama represented a time with hardly an attainable or recognizable trace remaining, a huge chunk of my life gone forever, echoed in this lament on time lost:

وان تازه بهار جاودانی طی شد   افسوس که عمر جوانی طی شد

افسوس ندانم کی آمد و کی طی شد   آن مرغ سحر که نام او بود شباب

Afsos ki umray jawaanee tai shud

Waan taaza bahaaray jaawaydaanee tai shud

Aan murghay sahar ki naamay o bood shabaab

Afsos nadaanam kai aamad oh kai tai shud

Alas, childhood is no more

And so too that fresh eternal spring has transpired

That morning bird whose name "Youth" it was

Alas, I know not when it arrived or when it expired

—Omar Khayyam

Hangaama's name was so much more befitting of her than mine was of me. She represented a beautiful time in Afghanistan's past, whereas my name represented friendships that didn't even exist. However, the more I thought of her, her particular name and Afghanistan, the more my faith was restored in the ancient naming tradition. I was beset by a bolt of revelatory insight: What veritable weight there was in a name!

For a moment, I contemplated what Shakespeare might have been toying with in his lines about the concept of naming: "What's in a name? A rose by any name would smell as sweet." Or, "Romeo, Romeo, wherefore art thou, Romeo?" I used to marvel at my father who not only recited entire acts of Shakespearean plays from memory, but had a deep understanding of them as well. How I loved the sound of all the lines, although to my unsophisticated, untrained mind, they often didn't even seem to belong to the English language.

I wondered if drawing parallels between Shakespeare and my Afghan naming exercise was obtuse or clearly unfounded. I was soon reassured that on some level, my thoughts on the subject of nomenclature were valid since all Afghans had names of special meaning. While I thought that the topic lent itself to some sociological study, I dismissed this idea since I longed for something much more tangible than another linguistic probing or analysis.

How I missed my friendship with Hangaama, who was such an unassuming, devoted, and loyal person. I could always talk openly and unabashedly with her about my shortcomings. We would have fits of laughter, and would even ridicule each other, without ever feeling hurt. I was so weary, in this school, of weighing and dissecting my words in assignment after unending assignment, in and outside the classroom. *Where was Hangaama now?* I wondered. *When would I see her again?*

As I longed for my bygone past and friendships, I wondered if I was beset by skewed expectations and behavior:

او ندانست که در ترک تمناست بهشت   عمر زاهد همه طی شد به تمنای بهشت

Umray zaahid hama tai shud ba tamanaay bihisht
O nadaanist ki dar tarkay tamanaast, bihisht

His whole life the ascetic spent yearning for Heaven
He did not fathom that in abandoning every want lies Heaven

—Tabrizi

Try as I might, forsaking family and friends was not an ascetic achievement of which I was capable. The best I could do was to continue to try hard to somehow persevere in their absence. As I feigned walking purposefully on the paths of my small campus,

I felt a measure of relief that my high school years would not last forever. I mustered some positive hopeful thoughts about the future although I seemed to be running on close to empty. Trying to bolster myself, I was reminded of more worrisome fates and my life's blessings:

حیف پای که ماند از رفتار   وای دلی کز و نه آید کار

حمت آسودگی نمیجوید   شعله تا وقت مرگ می پاید

Haif paay ki maanad az raftaar

Waay dilay kaz o na- aayad kaar

Himat aasoudagee namayjoyad

Shola taa waqtay marg maypaayad

What a shame when a foot is prevented from walking

Woe unto a heart when rendered useless in pumping

Courage does not seek tranquility

Until death flickers the flame fitfully

I thought about graduation when I would finally be set free. No longer would I be compelled to hypocritically feign joviality because I would be reunited with my family. What a boost it would be to see them and how genuinely proud I would be for everyone at school to see these cherished people who had sustained me all the while. Neither Emma Willard's contributions to my analytical thinking nor its perspicacity in mitigating the plight of foreign students had bolstered me. My support had always come from a different and far more distant source. It was a tribute to my past that the supply of my emotional fuel was still intact, needing only a single spark triggered by family to ignite into a roaring fire of confidence, burning brightly.

Suddenly, an inner voice, less harsh and critical, seeking objectivity and fairness with personal accountability spoke to me:

چرا ز غیر شکایت کنم که همچو حباب   همیشه خانه خراب از هوای خویشتنم

Chiraa zi ghair shikaayat kunam ki hamchoo hubaab
Hamaysha khaana kharaab az hawaay khayshtanam

Why should I complain about others since, like a bubble,
Ruination emanates always from implosion of inner trouble

—Tabrizi

Perhaps I was at fault for never revealing the extent of my difficulties to anyone. Because I was unaware of any remedial system that might have existed, coupled with my natural tendency to exercise caution as opposed to brashness, I was concerned that vocalizing my torment might trigger a backlash, causing a bad situation to only get worse. Upon further reflection, I concluded that the situation was very complex and perhaps no one person was to blame.

Sitting, transfixed in thought, I looked up at the perennially gray sky between the tall celestial turrets of a huge Gothic building. A few leafless, gnarled vines of poison ivy twisted out jaggedly in aimless direction amongst the garish gargoyles. From the outset, whether from homesickness or alienation, I was like a Shakespearian shadow—a mere insignificant, invisible one without a voice, without a name, or a country. It was as if,

من گنگ خواب دیده و عالم تمام کر   من عاجزم ز گفتن و خلق از شنیدنش

Man gungay khwaab deeda o aalam tamaam kar
Man aagizam zi guftan o khalq az shuneedanash

I am a mute dreamer and the whole world is deaf
I am innocent of speaking as are people of hearing

—Shams Tabrizi

The Beatles' popular song of the time, "The Fool on the Hill,"
which echoed this theme of alienation, resonated with me:

Day after day, alone on a hill
The man with the foolish grin
Is keeping perfectly still
But nobody wants to know him
They can see that he's just a fool
And he never gives an answer
But the fool on the hill
Sees the sun going down
And the eyes in his head
See the world spinning round

To relieve myself of gloom, I attributed my condition to an
inscrutable source and force much larger than myself that the
poet decries as the predicament of man:

دنیا طلبیدیم و به مقصد نرسیدیم   آیا چه شود آخرت ناطلب ما

Dunyaa talabeedaym o ba maqsad naraseedaym
Aayaa chi shawad aakhiratay naa talabay maa

We searched the world over and unearthed no purpose
So what then can possibly ensue in our Hereafter unbeknownst

106

As this period of reflection came to an end, my mood changed while leaving the unknown. I became more grounded in the present and turned once again to positive thoughts, imbued with an underlying and ever-present survivor's instinct:

به سینه میخزیم به دنبال زندگی

Ba seena maykhazaym ba dunbaalay zindagee

On our chests we crawl in pursuit of life

I thought, whatever past tribulations, I was bound to graduate... Yes, to be most definitely a graduate of this esteemed institution, considered to be one of the most outstanding schools, if not the most outstanding school of its kind. Certainly this excellent standard was true in the intellectual realm if not in areas of emotional and cross cultural challenges of international students. I sighed with a measure of relief as I infused myself with some more of that precious reinforcement of yore that spurred unbridled optimism:

تا ریشه در آب است ، امید ثمری است

Taa reesha dar aab ast
Omayday samaray ast

For as long as the root does in water lie,
There is hope that it will fructify

—Sherazi

Mustering calm and holding my head high, I began to walk purposefully forward, quickening my pace to confront my next class on time, all the while thrusting any sound or fury deep down inside me.

*****

Sending their children to the US couldn't have been an easy decision for my parents. At difficult decision-making crossroads, we all wish for greater clarity, a special wisdom, and perspective—sadly unavailable to us at the time. Even as a grown man, my father sometimes lamented,

مرد خردمند هنر پیشه را   عمر دو بایست در این روزگار

تا به یکی تجربه آوردن   و زان دیگری تجربه بردن به کار

Marday khiradmanday hunarpaysha raa
Umur du maybaayad dar een rozgaar
Taa ba yakee tajruba aawurdan
Wa zaan deegaray tajruba burdan ba kaar

For the wise and skilled man
Two lifetimes are required in this world
One in which experience is sought
And the other unto which experience is brought

Unbeknownst to Mom and Dad, they sent us to a very different America from the one they left in the late 1940s to live in Afghanistan. Thoroughly immersed in family life and the politics of Afghanistan, with only an occasional edition of the *New York Times* or *Newsweek* to read, they could not possibly have imagined the extent to which America had changed by 1970.

My parents treasured their experience studying at the University of Chicago, which infused them with an enormous amount of faith and trust in America and the American educational system.

Knowing that eventually their children would most likely be headed for a better higher education in the US, they struggled with the question of whether they should send us abroad for college or high school. There were advantages to each. Sending us for college meant that we were likely to be emotionally stronger and more mature to handle cross-cultural and academic challenges independently. However, attending high school in the US ensured prolonged and more thorough academic preparation. Political instability in Afghanistan caused them to choose the latter since they believed we would be safer in the US. Remaining in Afghanistan could have meant being swept up by the turmoil created by the Afghan communists or perishing during the Red Army invasion, which occurred only a short time later.

As my siblings and I grew up in Afghanistan, there were social, cultural, and political problems to varying degrees for us to contend with but none of them were similar in kind to what Americans in the US faced in the 1960s and 1970s. There were no people of African origin in Afghanistan, so as kids, we knew little about the raging civil rights movement underway in the US. The Arab-Israeli conflict was a remote abstraction to me in Afghanistan since I had never heard anything about the small Jewish community that coexisted peacefully with the rest of the population there. Added to the racial tensions and the Middle East conflict was America's involvement in Vietnam and widespread protests about the war.

My *tabula rasa* understanding of America began to be etched upon for real after entry in the US in 1970. The sexual revolution was in full force, with its shocking behaviors, styles of dress, language and blatant bragging about casual promiscuity. Also disturbing to me was the endemic drug use in the country and the drug-related deaths of celebrated musicians and others. With all that was new to me in American society, trying to sift through what was real or not, or legitimate and valid or not was a confusing process. I questioned certain accepted behaviors that in society seemed to be taken for granted. For example, the pervasive crowds of people camouflaged behind the very same indiscriminate Christ-like beards and ponytails, attempting to bring about peace, seemed an overly simplistic approach to solving global problems. Also, singers rhapsodizing endlessly on themes of passionate, undying love often appeared to me as disingenuous and even deceptive.

3. Omar the Tentmaker

During the first month at Emma Willard, I performed quite well academically. Teachers liked me, and I enjoyed them and appreciated their constructive feedback and complimentary evaluations. But socially, I felt a vacuum and was lonely. I had no friends and few people called me by my name. At times, I felt I didn't exist. Recognizing that it was up to me to do something about my predicament, I set out optimistically one morning, motivated by the saying,

از تو حرکت، از خدا برکت

Az too harakat

Az khudaa barakat

From you a move forward

From God unto you a reward

I headed to the student commons, hoping to meet someone. It was a small, simple room consisting of a few tables, chairs, and vending machines. I was excited about having a real conversation and finally getting beyond the superficial niceties of "Hello," "How are you?" and "Fine, thank you," and other fleeting verbal encounters while passing people in the hallways.

I sat at a table and opened a book while spotting nearby a group of five or six students gathered at a larger table. I couldn't help but notice their unusual hairdos, all the same magnificently huge halo shapes framing their faces that I learned later were called afros. Their hair had a blue-black hue—a certain glisten and gleam.

How do they cut and trim those? I wondered. *How does every hair stand up so perfectly and evenly in place and all in the same plane?*

I was intrigued but feared the girls would be offended by my gawking. It was only when I looked away that my sense of hearing took over, and I became keenly aware that, although fluent in English, I was having difficulty following their conversation. They were clearly passionate about something and this fascinated me. They changed expressions after each serious comment, laughing in hysterics, and acting out physically in exaggerated, sarcastic style. Then they would abruptly return to the same facial seriousness. This contradictory display of emotions was incongruous and unfamiliar to me, and I found it puzzling. I wanted to be a part of their discussion to feel a sense of belonging.

I leaned over from my corner table and raising my hand a bit hesitatingly, said, "Can I ask you a question?"

One of the girls looked at me, tilting her head to one side and lifted both eyebrows in a bored expression. "Uh huh," she responded.

I asked, "What was…that about?"

"Whaa…?" she said, uninvitingly.

"Um…well…I…I couldn't understand. You all were talking about such interesting things. I was wondering…" I stammered.

The girl recoiled, jerking her head and torso backward with indignation as she mocked my ignorance and screeched, "This ain't no 'thang' we been talk'n bout!"

I was alarmed at what was an obvious misunderstanding. Confused, I began mentally tripping over my words. Maybe instead of opening the conversation with a question, I should have adhered to the Pashtoon polite tradition of

اول سلام، پسی کلام

Awal salaam, pasay kalaam.

First, say "Hello". Then, let speech follow.

I became mortified because I had offended her although I really had no idea why. I hurried out a question in an attempt to rectify the situation.

"Yes, well, I didn't get the part about the quota. Why…?" I continued hesitatingly, attempting to stop Damocles' sword from crashing. "Why," I rushed out, "did that bother you?" I repeated the word *quota*, trying to appear somewhat cognizant although I didn't even know what the word meant. This was not met with a welcome response either and was clearly

عذری بدتر از گناه

Uzray badtar az gunaa

An apology worse than the sin

I was beginning to wish I had never taken the risk of starting this conversation. If only I had abided by the poet's cautionary exhortation concerning personal association:

نگفتن ندارد کسی با تو کار   ولیکن چو گفتی دلیلش بیار

Naguftan nadaarad kasay baa too kaar
Wa laykin choo guftee daleelash biyaar

Refrain from speaking and no one will take issue with you
But if you say something, then bring forth good reason, too

"Say whaaaaaa?" the girl bellowed, unforgivingly at my imbecilic question. Then her eyes abruptly returned to their erstwhile bored expression. Unfortunately, my ignorance or perceived insensitivity was met with further mocking hostility.

Not waiting for a response, she jumped up out of her chair, slamming the back of her right hand firmly onto a cocked hip as she bludgeoned on: "Wheeeeeeeeere you *been*, girrrrrrrrrrrrrrrl?"

By then, I was so taken aback that I lost the nerve to carry on the conversation. I thought I must exercise control to obviate difficulties:

زبان سرخ سر سبز میدهد برباد

Zabaanay surkh sar sabz maydihad barbaad

A fiery tongue makes fertile grounds for ruination

I felt quite ignorant and could not think of the words to prevent further complication of the situation at hand. At around age ten, during a brief stay in the US, I became mildly aware of the civil rights movement. Since my parents did not allow us to watch

114

much TV, and we were in an all-White neighborhood, I had little exposure or background on this topic in the news and was too young to grasp the magnitude and gravity of Black history in America. Having lived most of my life in Afghanistan, which was void of this problem, I was not adequately enlightened. Sitting with this group of students, I tried to understand, quickly piecing together their signs of indignation, which I gathered stemmed from much hurt and anger. Drawing on the imperative of Sa'adi, which speaks to the urgency for empathy toward one's fellow man, I remembered:

نشاید که نامت نهند آدمی   تو کز محنت دیگران بی غمی

Too kaz mihnatay deegaraan bayghamee
Nashaayad ki naamat nihand aadamee

You who are indifferent to others' misery
Unlikely will you be deemed of humanity

—Sa'adi

I wanted to show these girls that I was sensitive and genuinely interested in what they had to say. Unfortunately, I simply could not think of the right words to respond. Instead of telling the indignant girl anything about my background or exactly where I really had been as she was asking about, I assumed that she was not in the slightest bit interested in Afghanistan, me, or where I had been. I said something irrelevant like, "Ummm...I don't know," and the conversation ended.

Reeling from this botched experience, I endured its uncomfortable aftershocks for some time. When I was quite young, my father detected my overly sensitive nature and often tried to give me pep talks to boost and toughen me up to mitigate my angst in unduly talking blame. In the vulnerable position of being outnumbered six to one and with a penchant for self-incrimination, I failed to apply my father's wisdom:

شیشهٔ ناموس عالم در بغل داریم ما   هر که پا کج می گذارد ما دل خود می خوریم

Har ki paa kaj mayguzaarad maa dilay khud maykhuraym
Sheeshay naamoosay aalam dar baghal daaraym maa

Whosoever steps dishonorably, we agonize and suffer
The fragile glass of humanity's honor in our laps we cradle and buffer

—Tabrizi

As I tried to recover for the next few days, I reasoned that whatever the blunders, all of us bore some responsibility for this catastrophic encounter. I opted to pause and put into practice a saying that came up in my French class: *Reculer pour mieux sauter.* As such, I strategized "to take a step backward, to spring forward better." In the days that followed, I convinced myself to be grateful since the disaster could have been far greater:

بلا بود برکتش نه

Balaa bood barakatash nay

The potential for catastrophe was there but not its bad consequences

To get over the incident, I socially distanced myself and plunged deeper into my studies with a hope that somehow, eventually, it would become clear how I might dispel loneliness. For the time being, I bolstered and consoled myself with some worthy advice:

رو شکر کن ای مباد، کز بد بدتر شود

Row shukur kun ai mabaad
Kaz bad batar shawad

Go forth and be grateful
Lest matters go from bad to worse

—Haafiz

*****

Academic matters continued to progress well, but I still longed for social connection. In a few weeks, I was ready to undertake a new venture and expand my circle of friends. As I did so, I gritted my teeth with some trepidation, remembering a time when my father winced on the heels of a bitter political experience. He uttered the words, "Keep on dishing it out. I can take it," followed by words muttered in utter disgust:

تف بر تو ای چرخ گردون

Tuf bar too ai charkhay gardoon

Spit on you oh gyrations of fate!

117

I wondered what propelled this next poet's exasperated and frightful plea:

چقدر شوق مردن است مرا   زندگی بار گردن است مرا

Zindagee baaray gardan ast maraa
Chiqadar showqay mordan ast maraa

Life is a burden round the neck for me
Oh how I yearn for death to come to me

I brushed his words off as exceedingly melodramatic. Thinking that I had recovered from my initial encounter in the student commons and had toughened up as a result, I assumed that the deluge of social hurdles was normal and that I would simply have to deal with it and adapt. After all, what was the burden of one more social adjustment to be tackled?

چه یک نیزه چه صد نیزه   آب که ازسرگذشت

Aab ki az sar guzasht
Chi yak naiza chi sad naiza?

When water exceeds the head's limit
Whether by one measure or a hundred, what does it matter?

I elected to make friends anew and reaffirmed to myself that one bad experience should not curtail others. I looked forward to the prospect of new friendships as I entered the small student union area once again. I approached the tables with a tinge of hesitation but reminded myself with cautious optimism that

کوزه یک بار می شکند

Koza yak baar mishkinad

A jug breaks but only once.

118

I glanced at the tables scattered around the room and tried hard to bury the ill effects of that disappointing first experience. But the tables and chairs were a visual reminder of an ordeal I could not cast aside because

مار گزیده از ریسمان میترسد

Maar gazeeda az raysmaan maytarsad

Whoever is snake-bitten fears a rope.

Entering the room, I noticed various groups of students sitting together and chatting comfortably. I envied their loud voices, which suggested familiarity, camaraderie, and solidarity.

As I pondered a conversation ice-breaker, I noticed from the corner of my eye a familiar face, waving her arms and motioning to me from the far end of the room. This girl always seemed to me to be one of the brightest on campus although one of the homeliest. But looks mattered less at Emma Willard than anywhere else I had been. Here, it was all about the individual's brains, as if these were any less preordained by God than were good looks. Likewise, because the girls were so bright, I concluded that family and ancestry did not matter much, since

چون سگ به استخوان دل خود شاد میکنند   آنانکه فخر خویش به اجداد میکنند

Aanaanki fakhray khaysh ba ajdaad maykunand
Choon sag ba ustukhwaan dilay khud shaad maykunand

Those who base pride in ancestry
Like a dog with a bone are making themselves feel happy.

This girl, I would later discover, had a personality that matched her looks. She had often brilliantly dominated class discussions despite the teacher's balancing efforts to include others. Her rants often bordered on obnoxiousness and were deaf to the cajole:

به خاموشی یقینم شد   که پر بیهوده میگفتم

Ba khaamoshee yaqeenam shud
Ki pur bayhooda mayguftam

In silence convinced I became
That verbosity is inane

My classmate continued to wave her arm, beckoning me. I was pleasantly surprised to be summoned to sit with her and her friends and relieved not to be the social initiator. My imagination flashed forward with warmth to a feeling of belonging, to a place I longed for.

"Hey," the girl continued to motion eagerly.

"Hey!" the girl cried out again.

Seeing her arms continuing to wave, I was jolted into reality and allowed myself to experience a slice of excitement rather than remain in an isolated-observer predicament. I approached the cluster of girls with an unassuming smile. It felt more like one of polite elegance, reflecting both pride and humility, like someone in a global diplomatic setting.

"Oh, hi," I said to the girl in a cordial voice as my eyes quickly scanned the table in an all-inclusive glance.

The girl suddenly went silent, like

آرامی قبل از طوفان

Aaraamee qabl az toofaan

The quiet before a storm.

One of other girls broke the silence and in a friendly manner asked, "What's your name?"

Before I could answer, the original girl interrupted and piped in, "Oh, she's Omar."

Her voice was loud, full of certainty, and then she broke out into a roar of laughter, nudging the girl next to her.

"Who?" one of the other girls asked.

My classmate continued. "She's Omar, you guys—the tentmaker! You *know*, Omar the *tentmaker!*" she repeated more loudly, laughing obnoxiously as her double chin transformed into a jiggling triple one. Her chest heaved rapidly up and down, gasping for the air necessary to execute her multiple fits of laughter, as her face turned various shades of red with the rush of blood. I could see that she was perversely enjoying her power and the attention focused on her. Her behavior disgusted me. I could not believe she had been accepted into this school, most of whose students were much classier and more sophisticated.

A few other girls repeated the name "Omar" with exaggerated expressions of its peculiarity and unfamiliarity. Then they, too, joined in with laughter. A wave of shock overcame me. I was stunned and thought, *What is she saying? Why is she calling me Omar? What have I done to her?* Is this some sort of friendly overture in disguise? If so, it feels like

د خره مینه لغته ده

Di khru meena laghata da

The donkey's love is a kick.

I was bewildered. I had never been mean to her. This could not be a case of mistaken identity. She must have known that Omar was an Arabic male name. She had even made some sort of misinformed connection between the Farsi word *khaima* or "tent" and its derivative, *Khayyam*, and my last name, Kayeum. But did she think I was Arab or Iranian? Almost no one had heard of Afghanistan, so it must have been that she thought I was Arab or Iranian. I asked myself why she would make fun of me and ascribe that name to me. Omar was not even a female name, and it certainly bore no resemblance to Trina. What was her motivation? Why on earth was she speaking so? The questions flashed without answers.

Still trying to make sense of her underlying hostility, raucous behavior, half-baked knowledge and ignorance of Central Asia, I wondered whether I should continue to dignify her comments by analyzing them and trying to understand. I was surprised she even knew of Omar Khayyam. But my immediate sense was that she was up to no good. A seemingly contradictory refrain neither consoled me nor provided adequate rationalization. She was definitely not behaving like a friend, and I failed to see how this enemy might uplift me:

دشمن دانا بلندت کند   بر زمینت میزند نادان دوست

Dushmanay daanaa bilandat kunad
Bar zameenat mayzanad naadaanay dost

A learned foe will raise you
But an ignorant friend will smash you to the ground

—Sa'adi

After some more thought, I concluded that her comments were perverted beyond comprehension and probably represented some combination of ignorance and malice unworthy of additional scrutiny. Certainly, addressing her, in front of this den of lions seemed particularly unwise. I was extremely offended by her insulting behavior but attributed it, at least in part, to extreme ignorance, and I found some comfort in

آنانکه ندانند و ندانند که ندانند   در جهل مرکب ابدالدهر بمانند

Aanaanay ki nadaanand o nadaanaand ki nadaanand
Dar jahlay murakabay abadudahar bimaanand

Those who don't know and don't know they know not
Shall remain in abysmal ignorance forever fraught

—Ibn-Yamin

Not having an aggressive personality, I did not respond to her obnoxious behavior. But her flagrant disregard for human decency baffled me. I asked myself, "How could such blatant cruelty or ignorance exist in this very finest of schools?"

The famous elementary school quatrain underscoring the truth and beauty of our common humanity buoyed me and mitigated the base behavior to which I had been subjected:

بنی آدم اعضای یک دیگرند   که در آفرینش ز یک جوهرند

چو یک عضو به درد آورد روزگار   دیگر عضوها را نماند قرار

Banee aadam azaay yak deegar and
Ki dar aafareenish zi yak jowhar and
Choo yak uzwa ba dard aawarad rozgaar
Deegar uzwahaa raa namaanad qaraar

The children of Adam are limbs of one another
Created from one jewel, each in essence, from the other
If one limb in life is made to endure pain
The other limbs shall never in peace remain

—Sa'adi

By now, I had the urgent sense that time was of the essence in making a getaway. With the sort of fight or flight response involved in mob psychology, I glanced around the crowd for as quick and unobtrusive a face-saving escape as was possible. I did not want to give my attackers any additional satisfaction. Noticing a bulletin board a few feet away, and with a confused squint, I feigned an attempt to read what was on it from a distance. I slowly approached the board and pretended to peruse the disorganized array of hundreds of bits of tacked-on scraps of paper on display. All a blur, unable to read any of them, I left the building.

My classmate and I never spoke again. I had heard of great friendships being forged in adolescence despite insults and contentiousness, but this offense was just too great to resume a relationship of any kind. I reflected on the notion that love begets love and hate begets hate, and although I felt more hurt than hate, I recalled that

دل را به دل رهیست در این گنبد سپهر   از کینه سوی کینه و از مهر سوی مهر

Dil raa ba dil rahayst dar een gunbaday sipihir
Az keena soy keena wa az mihir soy mihir

Heart finds way to heart under the dome of heaven above
From hatred toward hatred and from love toward love

This lofty perspective seemed too far-fetched to apply in this instance, so I reckoned the following to be more fitting:

خر عیسی گرش به مکه برند   چون بیاید هنوز خر باشد

Kharay Eesaa garash ba Makka barand
Choon beeyaayad hanoz khar baashad

Even Christ's donkey if taken to Mecca
Upon return will still be the same old donkey

—Sa'adi

My eagerness for friendship and impulsiveness had again overcome my initial caution. I should have suspected from the start, from the ringleader's insensitive classroom behavior, that the outcome of this social engagement would be unfavorable as well. My patient efforts to befriend were futile and summoned

125

up the image of the notoriously stubborn donkey incapable of conversion:

پیش کلهٔ خر یاسین خواندن

Paishay kalay khar yaaseen khwaandan

Abreast the donkey's head, reciting scripture

As I left the student union, it occurred to me that this unkind behavior had probably been previously encountered by many others who in similar situations on campus and beyond had chosen the path of avoidance in the form of a peaceful bid farewell. I thought of the Latin response, *Pax va biscum*, (Peace be with you), and its Arabic equivalent uttered when confronted by benightedness:

وَإِذَا خَاطَبَهُمُ الْجَاهِلُونَ قَالُوا سَلَامًا

Wa iza khataba humul jahiloona, qaloo, salama

And if the ignorant addressed them, they responded: Peace be upon you

—Scripture

For some time, the days went by uneventfully, but there was one encounter that was reminiscent of the darker past ones. Contrary to habit, at suppertime, I decided to sit at a different table in the cafeteria with some new girls I was fairly acquainted with. Their table had some free space but not a chair. I saw an empty one at an adjacent table, pulled it out, and swung it into the open space of my table. As I sat down, a voice bellowed, "THIS is the B-L-A-C-K table!"

The girl, with eyes bulging, was shrieking at the perceived deliberate egregious transgression on my part. Her high-pitched voice prompted a vivid déjà-vu. I looked up at her as she was glaring down at me.

Oh, how utterly absurd! I thought. *Here we go again with more drama.*

As I dredged up the prior unpleasant encounter in the student commons, a French adage came to me:

Plus ça change, plus c'est la même chose!

The more things change, the more they remain the same!

The hostility and crazy practice of hoarding tables and chairs struck me as completely ludicrous. I had never encountered such behavior by any group or subcultures in Afghanistan even though it, too, has been historically fraught with the problems of a pluralistic society. I wondered if any other such tussles had occurred on campus. No one had apprised me of any rules of engagement or nonengagement in these matters. The girl's blaring animosity prevented any further probing of the matter. Unsure who between us was the mighty or the meek, I gave her the benefit of the doubt for being both. Her reaction brought to mind primordial behavior:

ندانی که چون گربه عاجز شود   برآرد به چنگال چشم پلنگ

Nadaanee ki choon gurba aajiz shawad
Baraarad ba changaal chashmay palang

You might not know that a cat, when cornered
Will pluck out in its clutch, the eyes of a tiger

—Sa'adi

Feeling somewhat resentful but unwilling to fight, I got up and gave the chair a gentle nudge with my knee to tuck it back under the girl's dubbed "Black Table."

That night before bed, I was combing my hair while reflecting on the unpleasantness of the day. In contrast, warm memories of family and a blissful past in Afghanistan entered my mind. My eyes blurred with tears. As one rolled down my cheek, I recollected the symbolism,

لولو از نرگس فرو بارید و گل را آب داد

Lolo az nargis firo baareed o gul raa aab daad

A pearl rained down from the narcissus and watered the flower

—Baydil

Exasperated by social difficulties, I stared at my reflection in the mirror. Reaffirming that I was made of sterner stuff, I swiftly wiped the tear away, claiming,

این نیز بگذرد

Een neez bigzarad

This too shall pass

—Sufi poet

128

Remembering being told that God is merciful and does not inflict one with an unbearable encumbrance and seeking comfort, I softly recited the relevant Quranic prayer:

رَبَّنَا وَلَا تُحَمِّلْنَا مَا لَا طَاقَةَ لَنَا بِهِ

Rabana wa la tuhammilna ma la taqata lana bihee

Our Lord, do not burden us with more than we can bear

4. The Throes of Academia

من علم لفظی فهو مولایی

Man alama lafzee fa hooa mowla-ee

Whosoever teaches me but one word shall forever be my master

—An Arabic saying

Respect bordering on reverence was what most educators in Afghanistan commanded, enjoyed, and were accorded. Although some may not have been capable teachers, they were still typically placed on a special social pedestal. Students jumped up out of their seats at attention every time a teacher entered or left the classroom and ceased any conversation in deference to a teacher's presence or when one walked by. Although teaching methodologies were often very traditional and even archaic, there was still a premium placed on learning as my father recounted to me in a simple tenet passed on through generations:

چون بی هنری عیب است   آموز از هنر چیزی

Choon bayhunaree aib ast
Aamoz az hunar cheezay

Since not knowing is a defect
Learn from knowledge something

The concept "Knowledge is power" is reflected in the many everyday quips of children:

توانا بود هر که دانا بود

Tawaanaa boowad har ki daanaa boowad

Powerful is he who with knowledge is blessed to be.

—Firdowsi

There have always been great teachers, although their numbers may be few. Some of the greatest lived in ancient times. So great teaching is not necessarily a function of the times or environment or the outcome of putative progress through time. The greatest teachers in the historical spectrum, in addition to being highly informed, are uniquely blessed with an extraordinary ability to effectively motivate and enlighten their students.

Emma Willard was no exception to this truism. Here, for the first time in my life, I interacted with many talented teachers every day. They provided an enormous and privileged opportunity for me to explore with vigor my full intellectual potential. Although I had been in accelerated learning situations before, there were none with the same demanding intensity as I encountered at Emma Willard. Enrollment was only around 350 students and small student-centered classes of just four to five students provided the perfect forum for daily active participation, in-depth probing, and personal and intellectual growth. Classroom work, and especially nightly homework assignments, were involved and challenging, often of great complexity, even tedium, but usually satisfying in the end. Teachers were forever encouraging, guiding interactions masterfully to enable students to constantly extend their boundaries, promoting continuous growth and learning both inside and outside the classroom. Critical thinking and analysis were the basis of all Emma Willard classes. Examination and deconstruction dominated the learning process when I felt common sense answers might have been sufficient. Contrasted with my previous educational experiences, probing at Emma Willard was much more heavily stressed:

یا نه نه ، یا ده ده

Yaa nay nay
yaa day day

Either nothing at all
Or too much of it all

In classes, it was not so much about what we learned but how we went about learning and the insights we gleaned. Although this intellectual exercise was stimulating, it was not always easy or fun.

In contrast, Afghan children grew up for the most part seen but not heard. Listening to one's elders was common advice given and obeyed:

یعنی که دو بشنو و یکی بیش مگو   گوشی تو دو دادند و زبانی تو یکی

Goshay tu du daadand o zabaanay too yakee
Yanay ki du bishnow wa yakee baysh mago

You were given two ears and only one tongue
Therefore, listen twice, speak once, and then be done

During my first weeks, I found classroom situations somewhat intimidating, and I listened intently but spoke little, only responding when called upon. Being bilingual and having experienced a prolonged two-track educational system of English alongside several foreign languages, I was used to the inherent disparities that existed between my fellow students and me. I had always felt I was playing on a different field from my classmates whether they were American or Afghan. From the beginning, and by necessity, I constructed a healthy system of my own to distinguish me from other students of a monolingual background, which divorced me from the complications and pettiness of competition. This allowed me the space and peace to learn at my own pace, freely, effectively, and contentedly. Within this construct, I explored the limits of my potential, guided by the Afghan fable,

اشتر آهسته می رود شب و روز   اسب و تازی دو تک رود به شتاب

Asb o taazi du tak rawad ba shitaab
Ushtur aahista mayrawad shab o roz

A horse and dog run twice as quickly
While the camel progresses slowly both nightly and daily

—Sa'adi

In both Afghan and American classrooms, which were prone to competitive rivalry among students, I was always comforted by a foundational belief and perspective that

زبردست هر دست، دست آفرید   خدای که بالا و پست آفرید

Khudaay ki baalaa o past aafareed
Zabardastay har dast, dast aafareed

God who made both the Heavens and the Earth
A hand superior to each and every hand, He hath created.

A feeling of admiration toward those who excel in class was ingrained in me. Rather than the more common feelings of jealousy, I learned from them without envy or scorn because any shortcomings I might have felt were obviated by the sage spiritual advice,

با خدا داده گان ستیزه مکن   که خدا داده را خدا داده

Baa khudaa- daadagaan sitayza makun
Ki khudaa- daada raa Khudaa daada

Do not begrudge the God-given
Because the God-given are by God, given.

Since I was naturally timid, I became increasingly uneasy when called upon repeatedly in one class, whereupon I would always give my best answer. Then the usually not completely satisfied teacher would gaze into the distance, and with a quizzical furrow of her brow and a pointed index finger, she would quietly edge on, "A little more on that…"

Feeling put on the spot, I would wrack my brain some more, internally pushing my every limit and digging deeper for some other point of perspicacity (which was still not quite good enough) as I would get confronted with the same probing all over again.

Oh, God, can't she understand that's all I've got to say? I would inwardly exclaim in frustration.

Another exasperating situation for me was when a teacher commented that my power of analysis was very good, but that I needed to work on my weaker power of synthesis. I found this irritating because not only was analysis the much more emphasized skill in all my classes, but whenever I tried to synthesize or draw conclusions, I was cautioned against extrapolations, which were deemed too simplistic or overgeneralized.

I encountered, however, all the best elements of teaching in my first creative writing class. Initially, I was unsure about the quality of my work and dreaded being criticized for all that it lacked. Nevertheless, I had no choice but to try my hardest and toil away to produce work as flawless as possible for this teacher. I labored mightily over my first essay, and stayed true to a childhood lesson learned in my elementary school:

مزد آن گرفت جان برادر که کار کرد   نابرده رنج گنج میسر نمیشود

Naaburda ranj ganj muyasar namayshawad
Muzd aan girift jaanay biraadar ki kaar kard

Without hard labor a treasure cannot be procured
The prize is acquired by the one who arduously toiled

—Sa'adi

Tirelessly, I worked at addressing both form and content issues; that is, assiduously avoiding run-on sentences, misspelled words, and grammatical errors. I scoured the dictionary for spelling accuracy, the meaning of words I had chosen—debating internally if my subject had enough creative punch, and whether I had substantiated with sufficient numbers of qualifiers and concrete detail. Above all, I addressed that onerous task of avoiding any sweeping generalizations. I was so surprised and relieved when in the next class, the teacher flashed my *pièce de résistance* onto the classroom board with an overhead projector for all to see. How flattered I felt that he found my work so exemplary and worthy of showcasing to the whole class. On another occasion, he read my entire short story out loud, and in so doing, could not have praised me more. I was elated by this success, and my head was in happy clouds for many days as I even fantasized compiling all my work into my very own *chef d'oeuvre* someday.

Because of the genuine, deep caring exuded by Emma Willard teachers in both my intellectual and emotional growth, I was always motivated to do my best in return. I never cut corners or took the fast or easy way out of a given assignment because

عجله کار شیطان است

Ajala kaaray shaitaan ast

Haste is the work of the devil.

The genuine outpouring of care and enthusiasm for my growth from teachers was as if they were acting out the Arabic declaration below:

اولاد کم اولاد نا

Owladukum, owladuna

Your children are our children

Another of my favorite classes was French, which demanded the utmost effort. Although from my studies in Afghanistan, I was fluent in the language, my Emma Willard French teacher did not allow me to rest on my laurels. She spoke little in class and required each of her five or six students to participate and contribute high-level analyses throughout the hour, solely in French. Every day for homework, I had to read a portion of important French literature—a famous play, novel, or poems from the sixteenth century onward. Then, within the context of its historic setting, students would answer comprehension questions as well as formulate ideas and opinions to be expressed in class in French the following day. A major portion of class dealt with the in-depth study of twentieth-century French existential philosophy through the works of Sartre and Camus. The aim, among others, was for students to achieve even greater fluency to the point of thinking and speaking directly and effortlessly in French at elevated levels. To further our fluency goal in French, we even used the Larousse French to French rather than a French to English dictionary.

For fun, I would listen to scores of French music and thoroughly enjoy making out the melodies by tinkering for hours on the piano. I would also pick apart the lyrics using my French Larousse dictionary. While others might have found these activities in music and language to be tedious, I found them to be a positive experience. I was reminded of little ants that are quite happy going about their daily activities without interference by others.

میازار مور دانه کش   که جان دارد و جان شیرین خوش است

Maiaazaar mooray daana kash
Ki jaan daarad o jaanay shireen khush ast

Bother not the grain-carrying ant
For he has a soul and the sweet soul is happy

—Sa'adi

One of my best classes was art history in which the instructor taught me far more than just an appreciation of art. Through her, I strengthened my communication skills, powers of analysis, description, comparing and contrasting. There was a very specific lexicon to assimilate which was foreign to me and very difficult at first. Lost in class initially, I scheduled several after-hour conferences with her to express my anxiousness and to get clarification and explanation of difficult terms and concepts. She reassured me that, in time, I would understand and to just use my own language. Little by little, with daily practice and many homework assignments, I gained confidence and a measure of skill in drawing on my own descriptive powers. In daily repertoires,

137

I began adding to and drawing from an artistic lexicon that no longer seemed opaque. I gained facility manipulating vocabulary terms in my collection believing that

قطره قطره دریا می شود

Qatra qatra daryaa mayshawad

Drop by drop, a river doth make.

In her classes, my teacher would flash innumerable slides from ancient to modern times. We covered the Mycenaean Dynasty, full of famous pottery, and I marveled at the sophisticated imagery on all the vases during this era. The terracotta earthenware connected me in a cyclical "dust-to-dust" primordial sort of way to my ancestral Greek origins and to humanity's life story. As I gazed at the beautiful shape of one of these precious artifacts, eyeing in particular its handle, a poem came to me transmitting a vividly humanizing voice into this relic:

این کوزه چو من عاشق زاری بوده است   در بند سر زلف نگاری بوده است

این دسته که بر گردن او میبینی   دستیست که بر گردن یاری بوده است

Een koza choo man aashuqay zaaray booda ast
Dar banday saray zulfay nigaaray booda ast
Een dasta ki bar gardanay o maybeenee
Dastayst ki bar gardanay yaaray booda ast

This flagon like me, a lover in torment, has been
Entangled in the hair of a lover's sweetheart, it has been
This handle on its neck that you see
Is the hand that once wrapped around a lover's neck, was meant to be

—Omar Khayyam

138

In all my classes, I was impressed by how expertly, and with great speed and facility, students would articulate their thoughts. Even in casual debates on subjects such as having the dress code or keeping Emma Williard a girls-only school, students would make remarkably compelling, cogent arguments both pro and con.

Most students were multitalented. Beyond the typical interesting classroom dynamics, there were frequent assemblies with very impressive oral presentations, brilliant violin and piano musical recitals, and dizzying dance improvisations involving expert spinning around a small stage while never missing a beat—let alone falling down. All of this made me aware of how much I lacked in these realms of excellence. It often seemed like

ترقی های عالم رو به بالا   من از بالا به پایین میترقم

Taraqeehaay aalam ro ba baalaa
Man az baalaa ba paa-een maytaraqam

Most people's progress is upward
I progress in a direction that is downward.

Even though I had positive feedback from teachers, I was exposed to such daily levels of quality performance that,

تا بدان جا رسید دانش من   که بدانند همی که نادانم

Taa badaan jaa raseed daanishay man
Ki bidaanad hamay ki naadaanam

I reached the point of knowing
That everyone might know I am ignorant of knowing.

—Avecinna Balkhi

139

I was unsure how to find the balance between asserting myself to get recognition while maintaining a measure of humility. Often this paradox seemed like

که حق خود طلبیدن کم از گدایی نیست

Ki haqay khud talabeedan cam az gadaa-ee nayst

Seeking one's due is no less degrading than begging.

While there were many outstanding students in Emma Willard, the rare and appealing quality of humility was harder to find in people of significant accomplishments:

گدا گر تواضع کند خوی اوست   تواضع ز گردن فرازان نیکوست

Tawaazo zi gardan firaazaan naykost
Gadaa gar tawaazo kunad, khooy ost

Humility from the haughty would be a virtue
A beggar acting humbly is already so by nature

—Haafiz

Of all the girls and faculty members, one girl stood out to me, and perhaps this was because she embodied the essential truth embedded in Haafiz's lines on humility. Anne Evans was soft-spoken and exceptionally multitalented but amazingly unpretentious. She was unassuming and exuded a rare quality of elegance in her humility. I had only a couple of exchanges with her, in which her benevolence shone splendidly. I wished I had befriended her and gotten to know her better.

5. Lofty Explorations

Over time, because of all the assignments and mental gymnastics, a state of ennui emerged in me as an intellectual void slowly began to set in. My academic enthusiasm diminished as I questioned where all this education was leading. Where was the objective truth? Was there even an objective truth, and if so, what was it? I felt I was working hard but without clarity of direction or purpose. None of my classes seemed to address this dilemma or speak to the emptiness I was feeling.

It was 1970 and the computer age was dawning. A young teacher was hired to offer an elective course called "Cybernetics." Fascinated, I enrolled, hoping that this new class would answer some of my burning existential questions. Listening to the teacher's introduction, I was drawn to his complex ideas that were novel and fascinating although often above my comprehension. I did not have a substantive mathematical background, which would have been preferred, but I was reassured by the teacher that it was not required. On the board, he began with many diagrams of circles upon circles and concentric circles, and I was focused on each one of them as I concentrated. His probing lectures resonated with me. At first, he seemed to address head-on the very questions for which I was searching answers such as, "What was at the center or core of the universe?" "What was the prime mover of all things?"

As he paced back and forth, he asked, "Was it physics, mathematics, religion, or philosophy?" In his lectures he would discuss computers, black holes, mathematical calculations of bits of information and all of what eventually evolved into a hodgepodge and blur of information that was hard for me to make clear sense of, much less apply in some meaningful way to things I could relate to.

Although fascinating questions were asked, I began to feel this course was nebulous and far-fetched, and my expectations for concrete results and answers were unrealistic. It was a course out of sync with Dad's counsel and approach. After undergoing tedious mental gymnastics and probing analyses, he would often shift the conversation into a humorous orbit to provide relief and perspective:

تو کار زمین را نیکو ساختی   که بر آسمانها بپرداختی

Too kaaray zameen raa nayko saakhtee
Ki bar aasmaanhaa bipardaakhtee?

Have you done justice to earthly endeavors
To now embark upon stratospheric adventures?

Cybernetics class was an invitation and an introduction for me into the fascinating realm of the unknown—a completely incomprehensible vastness, thus depicted in Scripture:

كُلٌّ فِي فَلَكٍ يَسْبَحُونَ

Kulun fee falakin yasbahoon

All is swimming within the galaxies

However, by the end of the course, cybernetics felt to me more like, "All was swirling in oblivion!"

Religion was briefly touched upon by my cybernetics teacher in his first lecture about the fundamental truth at the core of all matters in the universe. In my eager but ignorant thinking, I was actually hoping there might be an answer to this question but not coming across any definitive answer, I harkened back to religious sayings which eluded me in my Afghan secondary school theology class, for which I would seek translation from my father who had a deep knowledge of Scripture:

مِنْ يَهْدِهِ اللَّه فَ لَا مُضِلَّ لَهُ ، وَمَنْ يُضْلِلْ فَ لَا هَادِيَ لَهُ

Man yahdi hilahu fala mudila lahoo wa man yudlil fa la hadeeya lahoo

He who is guided by God will never go astray
And he who has gone astray can be saved by no one

I began to think about my own religious background. Although I did not practice religious tenets formally, I felt Muslim, and as all people in monotheistic religions, I believed in God, his omnipotence, and his prophets. My family celebrated religious holidays because of their rich cultural additions to our lives. My morality and sense of right and wrong was very simple and rooted essentially in doing no harm. It emanated from my parents whom I always thought were upright and practiced good, righteous behavior and expected the same of us. Dad always impressed upon us to draw on our dual background and to choose what was best from each to forge a better amalgam:

خذ ما صفا ودع ما كدر

Khuz ma safa wa da ma kadar

Take what is clean and drop what is dirty

—Yemeni Sufi poet, Abdullah ibn Alawi Al Hada

143

Toward his dream for a modern Afghanistan, my father encouraged a healthy dialogue between the progressives and the conservatives and coined a saying by juxtaposing two phrases to describe the two divergent groups of Islam:

اسلام مترقی اسلام قهقرایی

Islaamay mutaraqee, Islaamay qahqaraa-ee

Islam of the progressives, Islam of the regressives

Most Afghans were devout practicing Muslims, but there were many who did not follow religious rites and practices. As kids, we respected those who were religious as well as those who were not if they were good human beings just the same.

Like many children, I marked the month of Ramadan, the holy month of fasting, by singing this song as a greeting:

رمضان یارب یارب رمضان   السلام علیک ماه رمضان!

رمضان رفته بود باز آمد   بی نمازان سر نماز آمد

رمضان سی روز مهمان ما است   قوت دین اسلام من است

رمضان یارب یارب رمضان   السلام علیک ماه رمضان

Ramazaan yaarab, yaarab Ramazaan
Asalaamaalayk maahay Ramazaan!
Ramazaan rafta bood baaz aamad
Bay namaazaan saray namaaz aamad
Ramazaan see roze maymaanay maa ast
Quwatay deenay Islaamay man ast
Ramazaan yaarab yaarab Ramazaan
Asalaamaalayk maahay Ramazaan!

Salutations, Ramazaan, welcome Ramazaan!
Hello, oh month of Ramazaan!
Ramazaan had gone but has come again
Bringing those who don't pray, to prayer again
Ramazaan is our guest for thirty days
The strength of my Islamic faith, it is
Salutations, Ramazaan, welcome, Ramazaan!
Hello, oh month of Ramazaan

At the end of the month, with extended family, good food, and mirth, we would celebrate Eid—a three-day holiday commemorating the end of a successful month of fasting. In the same manner, we would enjoy a second three-day Eid celebration which came a couple of months later, commemorating the pilgrimage to Mecca.

Although my cybernetics class did not produce answers to my growing existential questions, it offered a refreshing shift by empowering me to ask fundamental questions rather than just analyzing the works of others.

As my sought-after answers about absolute truth never presented themselves, I wondered if a stronger personal religious conviction might have remedied existential questions, proffered solutions to my personal problems, or at least expunged my mental anguish in search of a more perfect and objective truth. Like many other kids my age, maybe I, too, would have been better off if I practiced a deeper faith involving praying more often, thus accepting Him more wholeheartedly to receive His blessings and help in my social adjustment at school. Words that seemed to emanate from the heavens might present a pathway to solace:

چون از او گشتی همه چیز از تو گشت   چون از او گشتی همه چیز از تو گشت

Choon az o gashtee hama cheez az too gasht
Choon az o gashtee hama cheez az too gasht

Turn to Him and all is yours
Turn from Him and nothing of yours endures

—Rumi

Ingeniously, the words *gashtee* and *gasht* found in both lines are in exact homonymous form; however, the two lines have diametrically opposed meanings: *gashtee* can mean "you turned to" or "you turned from;" "*gasht*" can mean "became yours" or "left you."

This witty and uncanny extraordinariness of words in both form and substance imbued me with a spiritual message that jolted me at least momentarily into undeniable confidence and belief in a sublime and generous Supreme Being and His gifts:

وَإِن تَعُدُّواْ نِعْمَةَ ٱللَّهِ لَا تُحْصُوهَآ

Wa inta udoo niamatallahay la tuhusuha

And the number of blessings from God, you cannot even count

—Scripture

146

I remembered, too, the powerful admonitions of teachers, quoting Scripture:

لَئِن شَكَرْتُمْ لَأَزِيدَنَّكُمْ وَلَئِن كَفَرْتُمْ إِنَّ عَذَابِي لَشَدِيدٌ

La in shakartum la azidannakum wa la in kafartum inna azabi lashadeed

If you give thanks, I will give you more; but if you are
ungrateful, My punishment is severe.

But alas, even exquisite scripture was insufficient to sustain unshakeable faith, and it seemed that working through my actual adjustment problems demanded more. I wondered if God had determined that I was ungrateful, and by disapproving of my fragile faith, was presenting me with scores of unsolvable problems. I shuddered to be perceived as thankless as there was no room for ingrates in Afghanistan:

یا قناعت پر کند یا خاک گور

Yaa qinaa-at pur kunad yaa khaakay gore

Either content you shall be or deep in a grave buried be

I found comfort in one of Omar Khayyam's somewhat brazen dialogues with the Almighty, as he tried to sort out his deficiencies and dilemma on faith:

وان کس که گناه نکرد چون زیست بگو ناکرده گناه در جهان کیست بگو

پس فرق میان من و تو چیست بگو من بد کنم و تو بد مکافات دهی

Naakarda gunaa dar jahaan keest bigo

Waan kas ki gunaa nakard choon zeest bigo

Man bad kunam o too bad makaafaat dihee

Pas farq miyaanay man o too cheest bigo?

Who in this world has not sinned, tell me?

And just how has he who has not sinned lived, tell me?

Should I transgress and You retaliate with retribution

Hence how do You and I differ, tell me?

—Omar Khayyam

Or this dialogue culminating in blasphemy and brimming with the shortcomings of human imperfection:

بر من در عیش را ببستی ربی ابریق می مرا شکستی ربی

مگر تو مستی ربی خاکم به دهن

Ibreeqay mai maraa shikastee rabee

Bar man daray aish raa bibastee rabee

Khaakam ba dahan

Magar too mastee rabee

My jug full of spirits, You shattered, oh Lord

The door to pleasure You slammed shut on me, oh Lord

Kicking dirt in my mouth

Could it be You who is the drunken one, oh Lord?

—Omar Khayyam

148

A few times when social or academic problems seemed insurmountable and feeling helpless to mend my situation, I entered a humbling phase of quiet desperation when my pleas gave way to more fervent beseeching. An even stronger supplication still failed to provide enough solace. Perhaps a stronger devotion, some even deeper amount of suffering or atonement for culpability, or a combination of all three was needed for me to submit entirely to the entreaty:

چه کنی جز این که نخوانی ام   تو کریم مطلق و من گدا

به کجا روم چو برانی ام   در دیگری بنما که من

Too kareemay mutlaq o man gadaa

Chi kunee juz een ki nakhwaanee am

Daray deegaray binumaa ki man

Ba kujaa rawam choo biraanee- am

You are Ultimate Kindness and I, a beggar

So what choice have you but to accept me

Reveal to me another door

For where can I turn if you banish me?

—Baydil

Not deriving sufficient peace from any of these repartees, and seeking closure, I dismissed all dialogues and resigned myself to the unknown with this wishful prayer:

خدایا چنان کن سرانجام کار   تو خشنود باشی و ما رستگار

Khudaayaa chunaan kun saranjaamay kaar

Too khushnood baashee o maa rastagaar

Oh God I pray when our work is done

You be satisfied, and for us salvation be won

149

Years later, during a decade of teaching young girls in Saudi Arabia, I traveled to Mecca. I arrived at the doors of the iconic Haramay Shareef Grand Mosque at dusk, my favorite time of the day. The rising moon in the sky was a mere sliver. Sandwiched between two of the mosque minarets, I could almost touch it. The ephemeral, fast-fading daylight dimmed, and a few stars became visible as the *muazzin's* beautiful *aazaan* or call to prayer filled the air, beckoning me to the dusk prayer. Religious thoughts, just as I had entertained at Emma Willard, passed through my mind. I waited at the entrance while an official guide made up her mind and then stood aside, permitting me to enter. As I passed in and gazed at the scene before me, I was in complete awe of where my life's journey had brought me almost half a century later. Many of my adolescent problems had since vanished, replaced by new ones. Soul searching spiritual thoughts of worthiness and doing good flashed through my mind, dramatized in that moment. I was grateful not to have experienced the following:

به طواف کعبه رفتم به حرم رهم ندادند   تو بیرون در چه کردی که درون خانه آیی

Ba tawaafay Ka'aba raftam ba haram raham nadaadand
Too biroonay dar chi kardee ki daroonay khaana aa-ee

I went to circle the Ka'aba and received no entry permission
What have you done outside these doors to deserve inner sanctum admission?

—Iraqi

Since I was afforded an effortless glide into the mosque, I felt blessed that I had passed God's test legitimizing my entry. I was lucky to quickly find a small space to sit amongst the crowd on the marble floor just a few yards away from the holy Ka'aba where once the Prophet prayed. I was overwhelmed by the grandeur of the moment and the mass of humanity gathered, united in the all-reaching common cause for prayer. So moved was I by this experience of the inner sanctum and so overcome by both the natural and spiritual beauty enveloping me that tears I could not explain began to flow. I prayed for the afflicted people I knew and wept for a while. As I continued to sit, I felt enveloped in peace and tranquility for the rest of the evening by the essential beauty and purity of Islam—and indeed, all religions—as this truism clarifies and underscores:

هر عیب که هست در مسلمانی ماست   اسلام به ذات خود ندارد عیبی

Islam ba zaatay khud nadaarad aibay
Har aibay ki hast dar musulmaanee-ay maast

Islam in its essence has no imperfections
Any defect therein is in our flawed perceptions

6. Riding the Wave

During my first term at Emma Willard, I got a welcome surprise when I found out that my father was going to address the UN General Assembly on its anniversary. Both my parents would be arriving soon and would visit my siblings and me for a weekend. I was overjoyed at the thought of this reunion.

Dad, greeting me in 1970, during first semester at Emma Willard after he had addressed the UN General Assembly in New York City

Once my parents and younger sister arrived, we drove to pick up my other siblings at their schools in New Hampshire and Vermont, talking, laughing, and enjoying the breathtakingly beautiful mountains full of brilliant fall colors set against a background of rich evergreens. The magnificent landscape before us was reverential and awe-inspiring, which brought to mind,

برگ درختان سبز در نظر هوشیار   هر ورقش دفتریست معرفت کردگار

Bargay darakhtaanay sabz dar nazaray hoshiaar
Har waraqash daftarayst marifatay kirdagaar

Green leaves of trees under the gaze of the discerning
Each leaf is a tome, revealing the Divine Being

—Sa'adi

My parent's visit was fleeting. Not wanting to spoil it with talk of my adjustment problems, I stuck to positive topics. But my father was wise, and surmising otherwise, used some of our discussion time to infuse us with strength and resilience needed to face any problems we were, or would be, facing. He injected words of advice into the conversation, reminding his young children: "Whatever your circumstance, you must remain strong, always ride the wave, and do not let that wave drag you asunder!" Although I did not open up about my problems, the force of his presence called forth this Pashto sonnet:

لکه ونه مستقیم پر خپل مکان یم   که خزان را باندی را شی که بهار

Laka wuna mustaqeem par khpul makan yam
Ka khazaan raa baandee rashee ka bahaar

Like a tree, erect and firm I stand my ground
Whether tis Autumn passing before me or Spring that comes around

—Rahman Baba

I was happy to spend this time with my family although it made going back to school harder. Adjustment challenges continued, but by now, I surmised this was simply the way of the world, and I would have to get used to it. Life in its very essence and nature was replete with challenges and involved unwaning restlessness. The sooner I fully imbibed what my father often relayed to me, the better:

موجیم که آسوده گی ما عدم ماست   ما زنده بر آنیم که آرام نگیریم

Mowjaym ki aassoudagee-ay maa adamay maast
Maa zinda bar aan aym ki aaraam nageeraym

Like waves are we, that in stillness is our passing
Alive are we because we restlessly are striving

—Tabrizi

By the end of the first semester, I enjoyed a stroke of social good luck by striking up a meaningful friendship with Madeline, an American of Asian descent. She had lived in America all her life but showed an interest in me and was more receptive than most to cultural differences. She was a thousand times better informed on topics about the West than I was. I tried not to ask too many questions as I detected in her a certain surprise in my gaps of knowledge in areas that were basic for her. She was extremely bright, and I was in awe of her facility and expertise at very quickly nailing a topic and churning out the creative writing assignments in her class while it took me hours upon hours to do the same. In the end, through arduous and assiduous toil, I completed my assignments as I was persuaded by

آری شود لیک به خون جگر

Aaray shawad
Layk ba khoonay jigar

Aye, surely this will transpire
If only through blood and sweat dire.

I marveled at Madeline's father's business success and appreciated his kind generosity in offering to include me on a very elegant dinner outing during one of his visits with his daughter.

November rolled around, and it was time for my birthday. I wondered if anyone would remember. Our family was rather big, and it was not possible to celebrate each and every one of our birthdays. However, around this time, I received a package all the way from Afghanistan. It was from my mother. With great anticipation, I tore it open and saw something that brought me to tears. I was overcome with emotion that she had remembered. In the box, neatly folded, I saw a shimmering white piece of embroidery, or *gand*, sewn into the bodice of a white tunic. The *gand* was exquisite embroidery work made famous by the women of Kandahar, my birthplace, and I had always wanted one.

Instead of being happy, however, I cried silently in my room. As usual, poetry came to my rescue, providing an outlet that consoled me. As varied stanzas came to mind, I felt better being connected to the beautiful words and infinite wisdom of the great poets of yore. Even though depicting sadness, reciting the bittersweet lines in themes laced with the concept of "pleasure in pain" was all very cathartic, soothing my emotions and rendering them not just tolerable but enjoyable. I began to feel better since, unlike the New England transcendentalists I had been studying who trumpeted ultimate self-reliance, I submitted to a power beyond myself and thus lightened my burden. I remembered a song that my father used to sing:

چین بر جبین نهاده در اندوه کیستی   ای آبشار نوحه گر از بهر چیستی

دردت چه درد بود که چون من تمام شب   سر را به سنگ میز دی و میگریستی

Ai aabshaar nowhagar az bahray cheestee
Cheen bar jabeen nihaada dar andoy keestee
Dardat chi dard bood ki choon man tamaamay shab
Sar raa ba sang mayzadee o maygireestee

Oh wailing waterfall about what is your being?
With wrinkles on your brow furrowing, over whom are you agonizing?
What awesome pain did you endure when all night long just like me
You'd hammer your head against stone, and weep incessantly.

With homesickness weighing heavily on me, I thought of these lines, even though I didn't act on them:

سینه میگوید که من تنگ آمدم فریاد کن   ناله را هر چند میخواهم که پنهان برکشم

Naala raa har chand maykhwaaham ki pinhaan bar kasham
Seena maygoyad ki man tang aamadam faryaad kun

No matter how much I suppress ululation
The chest says, "I have tightness... Cry out!"

As the night continued, I longed for home:

صبح میخندد و من میگریم   شب وصل تو به پایان آمد

Shabay waslay too ba paayaan aamad
Sob maykhandad o man maygiryam

The night with you is ending
Morning is laughing and I am crying

156

I folded up my present and laid it on my bed. My thoughts turned to Sohraab, the famous tragic figure in the epic poem *Shahnama* by Firdowsi. Sohraab was lying on a battlefield, with a fatal stab wound by his father who did not know that his opponent was his son. As Sohraab lay dying, help never arrived. In actuality, the poet laureate Firdowsi also died, never receiving his reward from Sultan Mahmoud Ghaznawi for the challenge of completing the epic poem in his praise. Both Sohraab and Firdowsi met their fateful deaths, memorialized in these lines which are often quoted in instances of painful untimeliness when a solution arrives too late:

زر فرستادن محمود بدان می ماند   نوشدارو که پس از مرگ به سهراب رسید

Zar firistaadanay Mahmoud badaan maymaanad
Noshdaaroo ki pas az marg ba Sohraab raseed

Mahmoud's compensation of gold is the same
As the antidote which after Sohraab's death belatedly came

—Firdowsi

I put my present in the dresser drawer, and the glistening white embroidery faded out of sight. While I lay in bed, thoughts of home and family soon lulled me to sleep.

III. Ascension

1. Love and Passion

At Emma Willard, I encountered little talk in or out of class about love, and not much of anything on this topic was referenced in the syllabi. I was bewildered that throughout my progressive education, this important universal theme appeared in none of the classics we read except for some treatment in the plays of Molière and Corneille in their depictions of the conflict between *l'amour et le devoir* (love and duty). I was intrigued by one comment and play on words of Pascal that I came across:

Le coeur a la raison que la Raison ne connaît pas.

The heart has reason that Reason does not understand.

This challenged the very essence of my education, which thus far placed all value on rational thinking and not matters of the heart. The closest, although still very remote, notion to a version of love I came across in any class was Captain Ahab's obsession with chasing the whale in Melville's *Moby Dick*. The main conceptualization of love at this point in my young life was that I would eventually meet and fall madly in love with someone, whom I would marry, have a family with, and live with happily ever after.

One of my rather jolting experiences at Emma Willard was attending a social event called a school mixer, when boys from Hotchkiss, a Connecticut prep school, were bused to our campus and welcomed into a hall to interact for several hours with the girls.

Within a matter of minutes, I saw girls and boys making out in corners of a room as though they had known each other for ages. The scene was particularly jarring to me, and I was shocked by this display of open physicality. Equally, I was bored with all the small talk at this social event. When a boy got a little too close for comfort, I firmly shoved him away. He became indignant, retorting how ignorant I was in not being able to appreciate this "greatest area of life," as I fled to a larger cluster of students for refuge. I never went to another mixer, since the experience, to me, was quite alien, unnatural, and distasteful and based on a flawed premise about socializing.

In sharp contrast to the superficiality of the mixer, I remembered asking my father about the subject of love and the extent to which it appeared in Farsi literature or its influence on contemporary behavior. Over time, he introduced me to and recited his favorite poems on love, which were full of insight and intrigue with emotionally deep and complex themes that were both profoundly serious and often humorous—and graphic as well. The nuanced sophistication with which themes of love and passion were portrayed in Farsi poetry fascinated me:

با من آميزش او الفت موج است و كنار   در كنار من و پيوسته گريزان از من

Baa man aamaizishay o olfatay mowj ast o kinaar
Dar kinaaray man o paiwasta gurayzaan az man

For me she is the mixture of fondness between waves and shore
Ever so close to me yet forever fleeing from me

—Kaashaani

162

دلگشا بی یار زندان بلاست   هر کجا یار است ، آنجا دلگشاست

Dilkushaa bay yaar zindaanay balaast
Har kujaa yaar ast, aanjaa dilkushaast

A palace without one's love is a hellish imprisonment
Wheresoever is one's love, there is one's palace

The summer before leaving for the States, I began reading with great interest. After completing three requirements for my French summer reading list, I elected to read on my own a novel that I stumbled across in my parent's home library.

Jane Eyre turned out to be a great choice. For the first time, I couldn't put the book down until I finished it. As a young girl, I had lofty fantasies about the perfect romance, stemming perhaps from what I perceived to be the perfect marriage of my parents, who were deeply in love. With their paradigm in mind, reading the passionate build-up of suspense and romance in the novel appealed greatly to my budding conceptualization of love.

I became at once perplexed and fascinated because I learned that the Bronte sisters had little experience with love but entertained enormously vivid imaginations that prompted their famous writings. This intrigued me, as did Farsi poetry through which so much emotion is unleashed despite emanating from a society constrained by strict segregation of the sexes. How the mere sight of a delicate hand, a revealed dainty foot, or a single lock of hair could trigger such passion was baffling to me and made me wonder if what was felt was not so much a function of an objective reality but a figment of the imagination:

دی در خواب سر زلف کجت را دیدم   نیش عقرب به جگر خوردم و بیدار شدم

Dee dar khwaab, saray zulfay kajat raa deedam
Nayshay aqrab ba jigar khordam o baydaar shudam

Last night while asleep, I saw the hooked tip of your tresses
As if stricken by the scorpion's sting, stunned I awakened

Or, this scene reminiscent of biblical forbidden fruit:

خفته بودی که لبت بوسیدم   قند دزدی چقدر شیرین است

Khufta boodee ki labat boseedam
Qanday duzdee chiqadar shireen ast

Asleep you were when I kissed your lips
How much sweeter is stolen sweetness

—Irij Mirza

Surprising to me were the countless allusions to love and passion depicted in Farsi poetry although typically there isn't much overt display of these emotions in Eastern societies. However, the complexity and challenges of being in love are understood and forewarned:

جگر شیر نداری، سفر عشق مکن

Jigaray shayr nadaaree
Safaray ishq makun

If you possess not the heart of a lion
Embark not on the voyage of passion

164

Sometimes love's resignation and desperation were also described:

بی نصیبم زان لب شیرین مکن   هر چه میخواهی بکن بر من رواست

Har chi maykhwaahee bikun bar man rawaast
Bay naseebam zaan labay shireen makun

Whatever you want to do to me is fine
Just don't deprive me of those sweet lips of thine

—Iraqi

عاشق زار تار تنبور است   از نوازش به ناله می آید

Az nawaazish ba naala mayaayad
Aashuqay zaar taaray tanboor ast

From gentle stroking to lamenting
The love-stricken resembles a tensioned tanboor* string
(*a string instrument)

The unjustness and suffering of spurned love, and the longing for love, have also been the subject of poetry:

ما سیاه بختان مگر فرزند آدم نیستیم   وصل آن شیرین گندمگون نصیب ما نشد

Waslay aan shireenay gandumgoon naseebay maa nashud
Maa siaa bakhtaan, magar farzanday aadam naystaym?

Joining that sweet tanned beauty was not in our destiny
But are we ill-fated not also part of humanity?

پیرم و آرزوی وصل جوانان دارم   زیر خاکستر خود آتش پنهان دارم

Peeram o aarzoy waslay jawaanaan daaram
Zayray khaakistaray khud aatashay pinhaan daaram

I am old, yearning for youthful connection
Beneath my ashes burns a hidden fire

—Irij Mirza

For effect and intensity, the poetry was complex, metaphorically laden, and sophisticatedly nuanced with hyperbole. The three degrees of exaggeration, going from "slightly" to "considerable" to "extreme"—known as *mubaaligha*, *ghulo* and *ighraaq*, respectively, were used in all themes, including love:

ماه را با تو به میزان نظر سنجیدم   از زمینش به فلک پله توفیر کشید

Maah raa baa too ba mizaanay nazar sanjeedam
Az zameenash ba falak pala towfeer kasheed

The moon I compared to you with the scale of my eye
The balance propelled you from earth unto the towering sky

—Rumi

Nature and beautiful gardens were a valuable metaphor for poets when describing a vast array of human emotions of sheer rapture:

بهار آمد تو هم ای غنچه لب سیر گلسان کن   مرا گرد سرت گردان و سنبل را پریشان کن

Bahaar aamad too ham ai ghuncha lab sairay gulistaan kun
Maraa girday sarat gardaan o sunbul raa pirayshaan kun

Spring is here, you too oh budding lips, come tour the garden
Keep me swirling about you whilst the sweet blooms are left brooding

166

The universal theme of possessiveness in love had a special meaning in Afghan society. The "three Zs," *zan, zameen, and zar* (woman, land, and property, respectively) were cherished central cultural values. Protecting one's woman topped them all and was at the core of a vast code of ethics and behaviors that governed society.

In poetry, love's complexities of jealousy with undertones of possessiveness were often depicted:

دلا به باغ مرو من ز رشک میمیرم   شکوفهٔ بادام چشمها دارد

Dilaa ba baagh marow man zi rashk maymeeram
Shukoofay baadaam chishimhaa daarad

Oh beloved, shun the garden for of jealousy I might die
Since the almond blossoms there have an eye

I often thought about the overall contradiction between Afghan poetry and reality and wondered how so much passion could spring from so little contact with the opposite sex in conservative societies. These were poets writing quite explicitly about the rapture of love, and were living among men like my conservative grandfather who forbade his wife to travel in the dark by the light of the moon to get to her mother's house for fear her face would be seen by a man. Although romance of any kind outside marriage in Afghan society was taboo, I wondered—as was the case of so many societies throughout history—if the forbidden was often acted on clandestinely and later discovered, giving way to jealousy and suspicion of infidelity:

ای کان ملاحت نمک خوان کی بودی   دیشب تو کجا بودی و مهمان کی بودی

Deeshab too kujaa boodee o mimaanay ki boodee
Ai kaanay malaahat, namakay khwaanay ki boodee?

Last night where were you and in whose company were you?
Oh, ultimate in coquetry, the salt and spice of whose dinner table were you?

تو که سگ نبرده بودی به چه کار رفته بودی   دی آمدم به کویت به شکار رفته بودی

Dee aamadam ba koyat ba shikaar rafta boodee
Too ki sag naburda boodee ba chi kaar rafta boodee?

Yesterday to your abode I came but a-hunting you had gone
Since this hound you had forsaken, why then had you gone?

Dating in Afghan society was unacceptable, and marriages were almost always arranged. After marriage, the focus was on a belief in destiny embodied by words such as *qismat* and *naseeb*. These words connote and emphasize that much of the success of a union or marriage was in the hands of God and fate even though we did our best to make the right or good choice. They were the underpinnings of matrimonial pledges and people drew on them when a marriage was in trouble. The words deferred at least some of the responsibility or failure to fate when a marriage failed. This lightened the burden of blame and defeat of the marital partners involved.

As an adult, I was struck by the somewhat random haphazardness of marriage, whether consummated in the East or West. All the unknowns in oneself and of one's partner, not to mention those that life hurls out during the course of married life (met with equally unpredictable reactions), drew me increasingly to those two inexplicable words of fate—*qismat* or kismet and *naseeb*. In my younger years, believing in my ability to control life matters, I readily snubbed these words. In later years, as the reality of unknowns in matters of the heart presented itself, it became more apparent to me that "the heart has reason that Reason does not understand."

As time went by, I was tempered and distanced from uni-dimensional truth-seeking, and I acquiesced to limited understanding in all areas including love and to the simple but comforting statement of faith, which compensated for mortal deficiencies, frailties, and failure. Although I would have liked more certainty and answers, I felt that I was more akin to

الذين يؤمنون بالغيب

Al lazeena yu minoona bil ghaib

Those who believe in the unknown

—Scripture

The state of being in love, involving all its wonder, vulnerabilities, surprising predicaments, and even surrendering of self, was embodied in the observation,

دل به دست دیگر دادن و حیران ماندن   عاشقی چیست بگو دلبر جانان بودن

Aashuquee cheest bigo dilbaray jaanaan boodan
Dil ba dastay deegar daadan o hairaan maandan

What is love, tell me; it's being the sweetheart of one's lover
'Tis to surrender one's heart unto hands of another and abide in awe and utter wonder.

169

2. Of Chromosomes, Yogurt, and Santana

Because of my different educational background and the standard of excellence at Emma Willard, I often felt academically deficient. I struggled with this shortcoming, habitually and arduously wracking my brain for originality of thought to achieve an edge of distinction. While remembering the comforting insight of my father, I knew that I was not the only one grappling with such issues. His words uplifted me, reassuring me that no challenge was insurmountable and that my trials had been encountered by greater minds than mine:

به فلک گر نرسیدی بن چاهی دریاب   یوسفی کن گرت اسباب مسیحایی نیست

Yusufee kun garat asbaabay Masihaa-yee nayst
Ba falak gar naraseedee, bunay chaay daryaab

Be like Joseph if Christ's tools are not yours to show and tell
If you cannot reach the skies then discover the depths of a well

—Baydil

One of my favorite classes was biology, although the lessons and concepts were often hard to master. I was repeatedly impressed by how easily other girls grasped theories and how they then leaped to exceptional extrapolations. One day during lab class, I was fascinated to observe cell reproduction and cell division through the processes of mitosis and meiosis. After much prior study and discussion about plant and human reproduction, it was

170

now time to actually see and identify the five basic studied phases of cell replication. As usual, a star classmate, Hollis, finished the numerous slide identification tasks in a snap. As I struggled to complete the assignment, Hollis took the class ten steps further than was required with her continually brilliant, if tangential, questions on genetics. Now she skipped into the topic of gene manipulation in relation to the concepts of isolation and aborting for the elimination of various illnesses.

Wow! I thought to myself, marveling at finally actually seeing some chromosomes after so much talk about them in prior weeks. I remember wondering, a bit perturbed, as I peered into the microscope, *I'm not even sure whether this is "anaphase" or "telophase"—and that's the whole point of this lab—and Hollis is already talking genetics. Boy, this class is way beyond me!*

I struggled a bit longer to discern what purportedly was an obvious differentiation. Squinting hard, I peered down into the microscope hoping for some clarity to miraculously reveal the two darn phases of cell division. I had difficulty deciphering these and felt like the dullard looking for his eyeglasses, unaware that they rest on his head or like the man who

سر خر سوار خر را گم کرده

Saray khar swaar khar raa gum karda

Riding atop a donkey, thinking he has lost the donkey.

Suddenly, not knowing the reason, I decided to abandon the urgency to analyze and identify chromosomal configuration between the poles. Instead, I began to simply gaze at these tiny black squiggly lines of life, marveling at creation and how such puny little things have persevered and endured the span of a lifetime on this earth. I lingered on the thought briefly, pondering their plight for survival.

171

Later, I completed the assignment, and soon thereafter, as we sanitized and disposed of the slides, a mortality question crossed my mind, more tangential than Hollis's concerns about genetics. How paradoxical and yet true were both the incredible fragility and the resilience of the body in the lifespan of a human being embodied in those tiniest of cells we scrutinized!

Just then, I heard my father's voice. I weighed whether I should share his words with my teacher. After hesitating, fearing she would find it completely off topic, I took the risk and decided to recite and translate a verse I found so relevant to our lesson because it miraculously connected us with the cells we were examining. She listened carefully and thoughtfully, gazing out the class window as I recited,

از سنگ سخت تر، از گل نازک تر

Az sang sakhtar, az gul naazuktar

Harder than a rock, more delicate than a flower.

She then turned to me in awe and with an expression bordering on bewilderment, uttered softly, "Ohhhh, Trina," and then more slowly, "That's fascinating!"

Whether or not she meant it, I was delighted that my comments had seemingly had the same impact on her that Hollis's always had on me. I left the class quite content even though I knew I had yet to fully master cell division.

For my biology term project, I gave a presentation on pregnancy and childbirth. As I researched the topic, I was struck again, more deeply than ever before, by the wonder, gift, fragility, and sanctity of life my father would unfailingly underscore through a life-exalting couplet that captured the essence and glory of creation:

هر نفسی که فرو می رود ممد حیاتست و چون برمی آید مفرح ذات

Har nafasay ki firo mayrawad mumiday haiyaat ast
Wa choon bar mayaayad mufarahay zaat

Every breath inhaled is life-promoting
And when exhaled is life's essence exhilarated

—Sa'adi

*****

During the first couple of months, making friends was difficult, but just as I gave up "waiting for Godot," who never seemed to appear, some social relief surfaced, giving me a bit of optimism and reminding me that notwithstanding unpleasant previous encounters:

سر زنده باشد، کلاه بسیار است

Sar zinda baashad, kulaa bisyaar ast.

As long as the head is vibrant, hats are abundant

I struck up a friendship with my classmate, Ceci, which quite effortlessly was meant to be. I enjoyed deepening ties with her, and this one-on-one approach to friendship proved far more satisfying and successful than trying to engage groups as a whole. Ceci filled up my leisure time and very enjoyably so. She was similar to me in terms of background. We were "half-American" because she and I were both born abroad and had only one parent from the US; both her mother and my father were from a foreign country. Although Venezuela and Afghanistan were extremely different, coming from dual backgrounds fostered rich discussions, and these discussions would forge an enduring friendship. Our ties to other parts of the world bound us as we shared scores of *tête-à-têtes* on the challenges of cultural adjustment. It was our foreign half that helped us open up to each other and sometimes even commiserate. She was cheerful and very pleasant to be around. Always complimentary, she had a carefree charismatic smile, so people were naturally drawn to her:

با نقلهای شیرین خود ، خود را نقل مجلس می ساخت

Baa naqilhaay shireenay khud
Khud raa nuqlay majlis maysaakht

With her sweet utterances
She endeared herself to audiences

As time passed, school was mostly enjoyable. The studies, exams, and papers came and went, and although the traditional A-F grading system was discontinued, my written evaluations were good.

At times, however, I grew weary of the Herculean academic rigors and my own very serious approach and deep devotion to studying. It had begun to take on a futile Myth of Sisyphus-like endeavor. Many of the class assignments involved the same exercise in mental gymnastics that had ceased to be quite as intellectually enthralling. I knew in theory how important the notion of balance in life was and tried to find other outlets as the Arabic saying reminded me,

خير الأمور أوسطها

khair alumoor o owsatuha

Good lies in moderation.

174

With her light and cheery nature, Ceci offered a refreshing balance to offset my seriousness. One day, I saw a difference in her appearance. She had a new and interesting look. The school dress code of uniforms had recently been lifted, and she, much out of the ordinary, was wearing an attractive light, maxi-length, navy raincoat over her clothes. I complimented her on this dramatic look, and she immediately encouraged me to buy one, too. I remembered my financial limitations:

چو دخلت کم بود ، خرچ آهسته تر کن

Choo dakhlat kam boowad, kharch aahistatar kun

If your income is negligible, spend more slowly

Assessing that my situation was not that dire, I tossed caution aside and squeezed money out from my school escrow account. Ceci and I managed to get passes and then set out for a store in nearby Troy where I bought another coat just like hers. For the rest of the term, she and I enjoyed our unique, sharp, exotic look as we promenaded around campus in solidarity, imagining ourselves, over and above intellectuals, as fashion trendsetters. How liberating this flight of imagination was, not only to have been able to briefly break away from all the intense studying but to be doing so as close friends. Probably nobody even noticed our new attire, but it was surely fun just the same to escape together from the restricting field of academia.

*****

In the days that followed, I ventured out anew to participate in a nonacademic activity held on campus. This was a great diversion for me from classroom rigors. *Oh, good*, I thought, *something different from all the studying, for a change!* Then I wondered how

I might participate, and if I could muster the ingenuity to contribute something of value to the student fair that was being planned.

What could I do, I wondered, *that would be unique and of interest to people?* My idea was to abide by the guidance,

پیش طبیب چه می روی ، پشت سر گزشت برو

Paishay tabeeb chi mayree, pushtay sar guzasht birow

Why go to the doctor; pursue past experience to prosper.

My experience in Afghanistan was that Americans were increasingly becoming interested in yogurt—a daily Afghan side dish—for its taste and nutritional value. I knew how to make it from scratch and surmised it would be an easy dish to showcase in my booth at the fair. All I needed was a big pot, a blanket, some milk, and a little plain yogurt for a starter. After unearthing all the ingredients and getting permission to use the school kitchen, I replicated the recipe and readied my contribution. I brushed aside any trepidation about how my yogurt would be received because I knew most Americans were unfamiliar with it. A Pashto proverb fortified my decision:

پیل په مالگه څه پوهیږی!

Peel pa malga tsi pohaygee

What does an elephant know about salt?

In my booth, I decided to add an assortment of honey, jams, and apple butter that I bought from the corner store a short way down the street because I thought most people might dislike the tartness of plain yogurt. The day of the fair progressed happily and the positive experience of students and others curious to try my creation, and their compliments helped diminish any unpleasant memories, which receded into time.

Another sensational experience outside the classroom came early during my first semester. It was the first opportunity for me to attend a live concert in America, at the nearby Rensselaer Polytechnic Institute (known as RPI). Often in recounting experiences, people will exaggerate the splendor of an occasion, whose reality falls short, as in

صدای دهل از دور خوش است

Sadaay dole az door khush ast

The sound of a drum is best heard from afar.

However, this concert far exceeded my wildest imagination. The booming, pulsating, exotic sound of electric guitars and African drums of the band Santana was exhilarating. This reverberation of sound was in direct contradiction to the notion that the glory and excitement of an event viewed from up close was less resplendent than it was drummed up to be from a distance.

The throbbing drumbeat, vibrating between my ears and the elation it induced repudiated the message of that popular Afghan epigram. Sitting in a small group with fellow classmates, with eyes and ears thoroughly engaged, I felt a newfound sense of affinity and comradery. I bobbed my head and marveled at all the flashing lights, repetitive African rhythms, and the thrilling sight of musicians at work. What a privilege it was to be smack in the very midst of such loud, exciting music and brilliant talent.

3. Reveling and Revels

It was November and my parents were still living in Afghanistan. Regrettably, I couldn't go home so I wondered where I would spend the Thanksgiving holiday. To feel a bit better about this uncertainty, although I didn't wholeheartedly believe it, I remembered that

خانه دار را یک خانه ، بی خانه را صد خانه

Khaana daar raa yak khaana, bay khaana raa sad khaana

For the homeowner, one home
For the homeless, a hundred homes

Fortunately, I was invited to spend Thanksgiving holiday in Ohio with my classmate, Nancy Sinsabaugh, and her family. They were kind and very hospitable, like many Afghans, who believe

دل باشد جای بسیار است

Dil baashad, jaay bisiaar ast

When there is heart, there is ample room.

As we drove through some of the cluttered Eastern states toward the Midwest, spaces opened up and the topography flattened, allowing full view of a brilliant sunset. To fully capture its beauty, I watched without blinking as the great big sun unhurriedly dipped and then slipped under an unobstructed horizon. Immediately, I was transported to the open desert spaces of Lashkargah and Laghman and to the poet's rendition of sunsets in them. For a moment, as I looked at the red-streaked sky, I thought about the ongoing political unrest in Afghanistan that my father had touched upon in our earlier visit that semester. I was unsure about the future and wondered if Afghanistan would undergo the tumultuous strife and bloodshed it had so often experienced in its history:

شفق را غرق خون دیدم نماز شام در گردون   مگر خورشید را کشتند که دارد دامن پر خون

Shafaq raa gharqay khoon deedam namaazay shaam dar gardoon
Magar khurshaid raa kushtand ki daarad daamanay pur khoon?

I saw the sky drowning in blood,
The dusk prayer in the air, a-floating,
But nay, could it be they've slain the sun,
Whose skirt soaked in crimson is sinking?

—Ayesha Durrani

My Thanksgiving stay with the Sinsabaugh family was lovely. During each dinner we sat around a big table, chatting and eating delicious meals. They asked me many questions about my background, and I felt very honored and welcomed. I learned how to make marzipan, which was very interesting, although I had not yet acquired an appreciation for its refined, special almond-flavored aftertaste. The warm Thanksgiving setting brought to mind,

قدر عافیت کسی داند که به مصیبتی گرفتار آید

Qadray aafiat kasay daanad ki ba museebatay giriftaar aayad

Comfort's worth is best appreciated by one who has been gripped by calamity

—Sa'adi

*****

Spring semester of junior year ushered in SATs, achievement tests, and anxiousness about college. I felt totally unprepared for it all. Having been in the States for only a few months, I was still dealing with numerous academic challenges and cultural adjustment issues. I was only fifteen during my first year at Emma Willard and was placed a bit randomly as a junior. This was suggested after I attended a few classes. I was flattered when the school concluded that, based on the maturity of my writing syntax, I should be a junior and not a sophomore. This meant even less time to adjust to high school before imminent preparations for college. The upside to this decision, I rationalized, was less time spent at Emma Willard before heading out to possibly an inspiring college experience. I quipped to myself, "All's well that ends well."

الخير فى ما وقع

Akhairo fee ma waqa

Good lies in this occurrence

Undergoing the weekend-long grueling, culturally biased SAT test was like nothing I had ever experienced. It was extremely intense and exhausting; I felt ill-equipped and overwhelmed. Many of the topics were unfamiliar to me. There were questions on global warming, carbon emissions, the greenhouse effect, climate change, and the like, about which I had no prior knowledge. The sheer volume of material we were expected to plow through in what appeared to me a fleeting amount of time left me feeling quite ignorant and out of my element. I tried my best, turning page after page and never reaching the end of any segment before a buzzer blared. When my head felt like it would surrender to my neck, it was finally over. The French exam, however, was a breeze and fun to take and the only one in which I performed extremely well.

180

By the end of junior year, with SAT exams, college preparations, and social problems behind me, my troubles diminished substantially. I realized my high school days were numbered and this phase of my life would soon conclude. I made the most of my remaining time because:

اشک یک لحظه به مژگان بار است   فرصت عمر همین مقدار است

Ashk yak lahza ba mudjgaan ast
Fursatay umur hameen miqdaar ast

A tear on lashes lingers but for one instant
And so is brief the duration of one's existence

—Baydil

With the possibility of moving to Cluett, a newly eatablished French dorm, for my senior year, a wave of optimism swept over me as I hoped for good luck to strike in making this fresh start:

بخت اگر یاری کند دندان ز سنگدان بگذرد   بخت اگر سستی کند دندان به حلوا بشکند

Bakht agar yaaree kunad, dandaan zi sangdaan bigzarad
Bakht agar sustee kunad, dandaan ba halwaa bishkinad

Should luck befriend you, a tooth could cut through stone
Should luck betray you, a tooth under halvah could crack

I was optimistic because the future looked much brighter. I even hoped to join one or two extracurricular groups to expand my social circle. I noticed the campus tennis courts—always empty—on my way to and from class and entertained the thought of picking up a racket and playing with someone. I knew sports and exercise would benefit me because

عقل سالم در بدن سالم

Aqlay saalim dar badanay saalim

A sound mind is in a sound body.

As time went on, I was joined by a few friends who all decided to leave the core campus to live out senior year in the French dorm. I was so looking forward to a getaway and change and to the peace and stability this move would finally bring into my life, just as

سنگ در جای خود سنگین است

Sang dar jaay khud sangeen ast

A rock in its place is steadfast and dignified.

Living and interacting with true friends, I would not have to suffer through any more awkward situations. Among this new group, blissfulness was guaranteed because even

مرگ به انبوه جشن است

Marg ba anbo jashin ast

Death in a crowd is a festival.

I was grateful for the hard-earned tranquility afforded by my niche in the French dorm, located at a distance from the main campus. I was completely satisfied just as a new Afghan bride would be during her marriage ceremony involving the henna ritual. This is a tradition of applying henna to the hands of both bride and groom and then wrapping their hands in a beautiful fabric while the dye sets and stains the skin. Henna, which can also be applied to the feet and ankles as well (and whose stain stays on skin long after the nuptial night has passed), is thought to cement the bride and groom's vows and is a symbol of their eternal devotion to each other. It is quite a lengthy ritual in a marriage ceremony, augering future spiritual peace and contentment:

من بسته ام حنای قناعت به پای خویش   دنیا گر دهند هرگز نخیزم ز جای خویش

Dunyaa gar dihand har giz nakhayzam zi jaay khaysh
Man basta am hinaay qinaa-at ba paay khaysh

Even if given the world, never shall I leave this place
I am bound by contentment as is the henna round my feet

—Baydil

Life in the French dorm was one of continuous enjoyment. We spoke French as much as possible as we engaged in fun activities connected to French culture. My interest in cooking, which started in Afghanistan, was reignited. It was a forte I carried throughout the rest of my life.

On several occasions, we cooked a full meal and invited members of the faculty to dine with us. We made from scratch a delicious *soup* à l'*oignon*, and *suprêmes de volailles* in a creamy white wine sauce, and on another occasion, a sumptuous *coq au vin*. We also turned out the traditional dessert, *crêpes suzettes*, which tasted delicious with tea. I took all of these recipes home to replicate for my family and they were very favorably impressed.

Ceci and I became roommates in Cluett and we enjoyed many lighthearted conversations and good times together. More than anyone, her laughter was infectious and even I became silly in her presence. I paid more attention to matters of a nonacademic nature. Every night before bed, I saw her applying creams around

183

her eyes, face, and neck. When I inquired, her brown eyes widened with apparent obviousness and then she laughed and simply said, "You can never start preservation early enough."

This made sense, and I wondered if I, too, should similarly cling to my youth.

*****

The end of fall semester was approaching. I was very happy, reveling in the ease of senior year and relishing all the distinction that came with it. Traditionally, one of the most fun and popular events of the whole year was the production by the entire senior class of a play called *Revels*, which was performed just before Christmas break. It took place during medieval times with all the costumes, language, rituals, and fanfare of the period. There were lords and ladies of the manor and many other characters and performances within this festive presentation.

The week of rehearsal was full of special traditions. It was thrilling for the entire senior class to be exempt from attending any academic classes for one whole week. Instead, we auditioned for parts and spent the time learning lines and doing everything necessary for the production of the play. We were not allowed to discuss any details with underclassmen. None of the younger students knew which senior was cast in which part until opening day. This generated a great deal of curiosity and anticipation, adding to the intrigue and suspense, which continued to intensify up until opening night.

During tryouts, something unprecedented came over me, and I took a radical risk. With an adrenaline rush, I suddenly had no fear and was not worried about avoiding failure or embarrassment. Knowing that senior year was going to end soon, and I would graduate and be gone, what did I have to lose? Tossing caution to the wind, I boldly thought,

چه حاجت با خرد هم خانه بودن   دو روزی می توان دیوانه بودن

Chi haajat baa khirad ham khaana boodan
Du rozay maytawaan diwaana boodan

What need to cohabitate with logic might there be
When two days wildly crazed one could be?

I charged into the audition room, quickly glanced over the script, and before a panel of drama department teachers to whom I'd never spoken, belted out with bravado my impromptu interpretation. Topping it off with a strong affectation of foreign accent, I set it apart from the interpretations of the other girls. It impressed the head of the drama department since I was awarded one of the principal parts in the play, as a lord of the manor. Over the next week, I mastered my lines and perfected the dance moves along with my "lady," who had performed in many other campus productions. This was my first ever part in any of the campus plays, and my bravado paid off because I enjoyed immensely stepping out of myself with boldness into the persona of another.

For the duration of the semester, I enjoyed friendships with some adoring underclassmen who were dying to know in what role I was cast. As they eagerly pumped me for information over lunch and in the hallways, it was fun and flattering to keep the "big secret," although it was very tempting to divulge. Instead, I faithfully hung onto the moment and savored deferred gratification in both me and my friends because

از خورده کرده امیدوار بهتر است

Az khorda karda omaidwaar bihtar ast

Anticipating exceeds the pleasure of having.

This romp went on for all of *Revels* week, and I was thoroughly amused as my little sisters fussed and fussed all over me. Opening night was exhilarating. As I made my entrance in full costume, it was thrilling to be pointed at and to hear my name shouted out from the audience by those underclassmen who had been so curious and managed to recognize me behind my costume disguise. I had shocked them, since hitherto I had had absolutely no involvement whatsoever in any of the drama productions of the school.

I wished my parents could have been there to see me in my full glory. This was a first-time experience for me, and I felt they would be so proud of me. Happily, Marya and Rona had left school for winter break and were in the audience to witness my accomplishment and cheer me on.

*****

Spring semester was zipping by. The remainder of senior year was quite pleasant. As graduation approached, Ceci and I tried to lose some weight to look good in pictures. She tried to cut back by snacking on Muenster cheese and appetite-quelling banana pieces dipped in small amounts of peanut butter and honey. I cut out desserts altogether, which had been my downfall. Our efforts paid off because we managed to shed a few pounds.

Graduation was planned and overseen by the principal's wife. It was determined that graduates would wear a long white dress and walk down the aisle carrying one long-stemmed rose, which I thought was elegant. I thought it a bit curious, however, to be dressing up in long white gowns as if we were brides. Nonetheless, before graduation, Ceci and I got passes to go into Troy to explore dress options. I did not find one since none of them were affordable or simple enough for the understated look with which I would be comfortable. Ceci managed to find a couple of possibilities to take home and think about. She bought them with a piece of plastic that she swiftly swiped and followed with some scribbling. This was the first time I had seen a credit card. I tried to understand how it worked with no exchange of actual money, but with her ease in using it, I felt I should already know and was too embarrassed to ask. It was somewhat irrelevant to me anyhow because I didn't have one. I knew I would not be buying a dress, and as the days went by, I wondered how I would fulfill the requirement of a long white gown.

By now, my parents were in the US. My mother offered to sew a dress for me. We decided on simplicity of style—a straightish, flattering, long white dress with a slightly shirred peasant-blouse neckline. I asked her if she could somehow incorporate the famous white-on-white Kandahari *gand* embroidery as an embellishment into the bodice of the dress. She determined that such an accent, sewn in the mid-section of the dress, would be flattering and quite possible. Mom pulled off the plan to perfection. She whipped it up during spring break, and I was relieved of any worries associated with graduation.

I invited Ceci to spend spring break with me and my family where they now lived in Larchmont, New York. It felt great to be the one hosting this wonderful time together. The remainder of the term, I enjoyed the kind of carefree coasting associated with senior year. I was already somehow in the future, looking back upon the good times at Emma Willard with nostalgia. Nothing brought me down, neither past hurdles nor worries of an unknown future.

As the end of high school was in plain sight, grateful thoughts abounded. Emma Willard had contributed more to my intellectual and academic growth than any institution, either before or since. I had always toiled hard in school, but this had been a time of tremendous receptivity, intellectual hunger, and personal growth. I had learned more in my two years here than anywhere. Thanks to the quality of education I had received, I was able to take several upper-level courses during my first year at the University of Wisconsin. I had worked harder at Emma Willard than I subsequently would, either in college or graduate school.

I was so proud when my whole family attended graduation to acknowledge my accomplishment. All concerns had dissipated, prior scars healed, and I was grateful for my education and achievement. My tireless work up until this day was by no means easy, but I had learned a lot, attained my goal, and had even made friends. Despite many triumphs, I knew there was yet a long road ahead to unlock my full potential because

صد سال سفر باید تا پخته شود خامی

Sad saal safar baayad taa pukhta shawad khaamay

A hundred years of travel it doth take for the raw, ripe to make.

—Sa'adi

On graduation day, I was buoyant and filled completely with feelings of achievement. I stood in line, symbolically holding the essential beauty of a single long-stemmed rose, and felt tremendous pride on this day.

My entire high school experience of dogged determination and perseverance flashed before me even though it was behind me as I beamed a genuine smile in all the pictures taken throughout

188

the day. I had diligently pursued and lived these words which now resonated in me as never before:

ز دریا می کشد صیاد دام آهسته آهسته به مقصد می رسد جویای کام آهسته آهسته

Ba maqsad mayrasad joyaay kaam, aahista aahista
Zi daryaa maykashad siaad daam, aahista aahista

The seeker his purpose fulfills, painstakingly slowly
From a river, pries out the fisherman his prey, ever so slowly

—Saa'ib Tabrizi

Revels play. I, cast as a lord, seated at table, second from right.

Holding a single rose, I walk in the graduation procession.

Dad and I on graduation day.

4. Reconciling Loss

During the last few days of high school, as I walked around my campus, I never fathomed that more than half a century would pass without even a visit back to my place of birth. Days, weeks, and months devolved into years, then decades, as expatriation seemed forever fossilized. Walking in Lashkargah along the two short streets that bordered my entire childhood world, or seeking a measure of peace in Laghman's pristine air, or even seeing places devoid of beautiful memories had become an impossible dream.

Wishing for a homeland visit brought to mind questions and the possibility that perhaps we do not always know what is good for us. Scripture calls out the sometimes stubborn and misguided longings of individuals and draws attention to the unknown higher order of all things that only God fully understands as stated in the Quran:

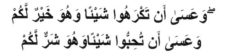

Wa asa an takraho shaian wa hua khairulakum
Wa an tuhibo shaian wa hua sharulakum

And it is possible that ye dislike a thing that is good for you
And possible that ye love a thing that is bad for you

To cope with uncertainties, I distracted and busied myself with thoughts of college looming and de-emphasized the unattainable or ambitious goal of visiting my land of birth. But I was intrigued by a hopeful and lofty Arabic axiom,

كل شيء يرجع إلى أصله

Kulu shaian yarja-o ila aslahee

Everything returns to its origin

In yearning, I was my father's daughter, duly observed in Arabic:

اثر الابا يظهر الا بنا

asar al aba yazhuru al abna

Hereditary traits of a father manifest in his offspring

Neither my father nor I made it back to Afghanistan after our departures. Sometimes, as he spent his life aging abroad like many other Afghan patriots, he wondered if he could eventually be buried in Laghman—or somewhere in Afghanistan—to be reunited in a way that was impossible while he was alive. I remember welling up with tears, along with my sister, when he referred to the inevitability of death and burial:

خاک وطن برفت چه خاک را بر سر بیندازیم

Khaakay watan biraft chi khaak raa bar sar biandaazaym

The homeland's soil is gone
What soil do we have to throw over our head?

Coping with the grim war-torn reality of Afghanistan caused me to wish for a globe that belonged to us all. I was both enlightened by and derived solace from the spirituality of a sonnet that speaks to living a fulfilling life beyond the limiting confines of a given national border:

هر جا ملک ماست که ملک خدای ماست

Har jaa mulkay maast Ki mulkay khudaay maast

Every country is our country that is our God's country

*****

After high school, I attended college and majored in my favorite subject, French, and then went on to Columbia University for a master's of arts degree. Employment in the US had taken a downturn in the late 1970s, and jobs were scarce so I went to Saudi Arabia to work beyond the confines of borders. Upon returning to the US, I met my husband, Ahad, also originally from Afghanistan, in DC, on a blind date arranged by friends. After a short long-distance courtship across states, I took a great leap of faith and agreed to marry him a couple of months later. Knowing that longer courtships did not necessarily ensure long-lasting marriages, I opted to believe in what fate had presented me with, accepting the Eastern notion of *Qismat* or *Kismet.* Surprising, if not shocking, to my relatives and American friends, including sometimes even myself, was completing full circle, in such a rapid way, this very Afghan cultural tradition of marriage. We now have a wonderful grown son, Kamran, and live in the state of Colorado, whose beautiful, blue skies and snow-capped mountains lie picturesquely before us, reminding us so closely every day of our beloved faraway homeland.

******

Many years after my marriage, I experienced my second greatest loss after country. My beloved father passed away. Of course, I'd always known of this inevitability that the Quran, too, reminds us of:

كُلُّ نَفْسٍ ذَآئِقَةُ ٱلْمَوْتِ

Kulo nafsin zaiqatul mowt

Every soul shall have a taste of death

However, losing my father, who had been my rock through life, was indeed difficult. To uplift me, I was filled with wonderful, albeit bittersweet, memories of him and our relationship. Still, the finality of death was baffling:

هر گل که بیشتر به چمن میدهد صفا   گلچین روزگار امانش نمیدهد

Har gul ki bayshtar ba chaman maydihad safaa
Gulcheenay rozgaar amaanash namaydihad

Every flower that delivers the most beauty to a field
Life's flower plucker does not grant it safety

From high school graduation through the present, I continue to oscillate paradoxically between Voltaire's Panglossian perspective, *C'est le meilleur des mondes possibles* (This is the best of all possible worlds) and his character Candide's pragmatism, *Il faut cultiver notre jardin* (We must cultivate our garden).

There are moments when I am optimistic about Afghanistan, and then there are times when hopelessness becomes overwhelming.

Yet through all the ups and downs, wise words regarding other equally dark periods in history still prevail and provide comfort:

اى دل صبور باش و مخور غم كه عاقبت   اين شام صبح گردد و اين شب سحر شود

Ai dil saboor baash o makhur gham ki aaqibat
Een shaam sob gardad o een shab sahar shawad

Oh heart, be patient and grieve not, for in time
This evening shall the morrow become and this night the break of day

—Haafiz

In spite of all the false starts and disillusions for a better Afghanistan, I have accepted an outlook that gives way to elements of both the optimism and practical realism to which Sa'adi speaks:

گر بماندیم زنده بردوزیم جامهٔ کز فراق چاک شده
ور بمردیم عذر ما بپذیر ای بسا آرزو که خاک شده

Gar bimaandaym zinda bardozaym
Jaamay kaz firaaq chaak shuda
War bimurdaym uzray maa bipazeer
Ai bassaa aarizo ki khaak shuda

If still alive, we will diligently darn
The garment that separation has torn apart
And if we die, accept our plea
Alas, all yearnings that woefully have turned to dust

—Sa'adi

Despite the pain and hardship that life dispenses, as in the experience of Candide, I am both surprised and encouraged that, within the limits of Pangloss's "greatest of all possible worlds," periodic, gentle, positive assurances, whose existence and origins are often difficult to discern, still manage to emanate and somehow faithfully and tangibly drift into my life: a beautiful day, a good night's sleep, a warm bed and shower, a culinary creation, a nostalgic tune, a pleasant walk, visit, breeze, or memory. Like Candide, I am busy "cultivating" my "garden" of blessings. These blessings can often be as far away or as faint as the ever-so-soft jingling of a single bell, dangling from the neck of some camel in a Koochee caravan as it plods its way painstakingly across a barren desert in Afghanistan. But blessings and assurances do exist and inexplicably auger hope for a more perfect world, if not on earth, then someday, in a place void of all earthly impediments:

ما را به ميان آن فضا سودائيست   از كفر و ز اسلام بيرون صحرائيست

نه كفرو نه اسلام و نه آنجا جاييست   عارف چو بدان رسيد سر را بنهد

Az Kufur o zi Islam biroon sahraayst

Maa raa ba miyaanay aan fazaa sowdaayst

Aarif choo badaan raseed sar raa binihad

Na Kufur o na Islam o na aanjaa jaa- ayst

Beyond Atheism and Islam there is a field

Amidst that empyrean awaits us a reckoning

The enlightened thereupon arriving bows his head

No Atheism and no Islam nor room is there for any such place overhead

—Rumi

Even though I always thought the loss of my father would be cataclysmic for me, unexpected feelings emerged as I sat at his funeral. Surprisingly at peace, I was uplifted by the rich life full of purpose that he led, so loved and recognized by all whose lives he had touched. I could not have asked for better or more in my relationship with him as his daughter. Within the realm of mortal reality, at the funeral, I was reminded of and comforted by the sense of oneness of all humanity, as expressed so well by the hopeful words of Rumi, and by the closing words of great solace in Scripture, applied upon death to all of God's subjects. Uttered during prayers for the deceased, these words consoled and continue to console me:

إِنَّا لِلَّه وَ إِنَّا إِلَيْهِ رَاجِعونَ

Inna lillahi wa inna ilayhi rajioon

From Allah we come and to Him we return

IV. Pronunciation Guide

Letters in the Transcription	Equivalent Sounds in English
a	up, cup, sun
aa	awe, on, lawn
ay	may, ray
ee	eek, sheet
i	is, his
o	own, shown
ow	owl, now
oo	noon, moon, ooze
u	put
zh	measure, leisure, pleasure
Sounds not found in English	
q	"k" (a uvular stop) qismat, ishq
r	"r" (as trilled in Spanish) raftam, buro
gh	"r" (as in "merci" in French) gham, baagh
kh	"ch" (as in Bach) khaan, malakh

V. Glossary

"Akhtar di mubaarak sha!"	"Happy Eid to you!" (in Pashto)
aalaab	long winded musical scales
Aashura	holy day in Islam marking the martyrdom of Imam Hassan and Imam Hussein
aazaan	call to prayer
"Bala dee wakhlam!"	"Let me assume all ills and dangers that could possibly befall you!"
Buzkashi	the national game similar to Polo
chaadaree	womens' full body fabric covering
chaar paa-ee	four-legged wooden bed strung with heavy-duty straw reinforcements
chaapandaaz	a Buzkashi horseman
chukeeda	mixture of ground walnuts and mulberries
dil-tang	restless
dogh	Farsi word for yogurt drink with chopped cucumber and mint
Eid	two three-day celebrations—one at the end of Ramadan and the other during the Mecca pilgrimage
firnee	a dessert pudding
gaadee	horse-driven carriage

gand	shimmering white piece of embroidery sewn into the bodice of a tunic
gasht	became/left
gashtee	you turned to/you turned away from
ghazal	a melodious song of lyrical poetry
ghulo	middle level of exaggeration
hangaam	a time
ighraaq	highest form of exaggeration
ismay baa musamaa	a name with meaning
ismay bay musamaa	a name without meaning
jilabee	fried and honey-dipped pastry
"Khair ast"	"Never mind; it's okay"
khaima	tent
Khayyam	proper name—derivative of khaima (tent)
Khan	head of a clan, village or tribe
khasta	tired
Koochee	Afghan nomad
lee-aaf	comforter
liwanay	crazy
makala makala	made-up words by children
muazzin	the one who makes the call to prayer
mubaaligha	least form of exaggeration
naan	Afghan bread
naan-baa-ee	bakery for baking bread only
nafas	breath
naseeb	destiny
Now Roz	Afghan New Year
paiko	water-run mill
payraan	long tunic (shirt) for men
qalaa	adobe fortress
qismat	kismet
raga	an ancient melodic pattern in Indian music

Ramadan	month of fasting—pronounced "Ramazaan" in Afghanistan
"Sadqayt shawam!"	"May I be sacrificed for you!"
sandalee	a small metal heater under a table covered with comforters
saraay	shopping alleyway
Shia	one of the two main sects in Islam
shlombay	Pashto word for yogurt drink with chopped cucumber and mint
tabla chi	drummer
taghaara	large earthenware
takya khaana	Shia religious centers
tanboor	a string instrument
tandor	deep oven in the ground
toshak	thin mattress
tunbaan (written but pronounced "tumbaan")	Afghan baggy pants
ustaad	a professional musician, teacher, or professor
Waadee Helmand	The Helmand Valley
waaskat	vest
wilaayat	province
zameen	land
zan	woman
zar	gold

Lightning Source UK Ltd.
Milton Keynes UK
UKHW020642010223
416289UK00011B/220